S0-DXN-215

Karemina-Girl-small
Ulla
Dominique - Boy

Colourpoint Longhair
and
Himalayan Cats

Colorpoint Longhair
&
Himalayan Cats

GENETICS, BREEDING AND CARE OF THESE AND OTHER PEDIGREE CATS

S. M. MANTON (Mrs. J. P. Harding)
F.R.S.

CROWN PUBLISHERS, INC.
NEW YORK

© George Allen & Unwin Ltd., 1971

First published in the United States
of America 1971 by Crown Publishers, Inc.
Library of Congress Catalog Card No : 78-148086

Printed in Great Britain
in 10 on 12 point Times
BY BLACKFRIARS PRESS LTD.
LEICESTER

Preface

The following pages and illustrations have been prepared in response to the rapid increase in interest in pedigree cats all over the world, and to the consequent demand for information of a precise nature. In particular the numbers of Colourpoint (Himalayan) cats are growing at a rate which may soon make them the most popular variety of feline pet. Both breeders and owners of these cats have no suitable book of reference and the need is keenly felt.

The technical information recorded is minimal and presented in such a way as to be readily understandable by anyone wishing to read, but possessing no previous specialized knowledge. The scientific basis of animal breeding, and the relationship of one domestic variety to another are clearly and simply explained on a practical basis, such as is needed by the interested public. Owners and breeders alike are provided with working details concerning breeding and maintenance. Some information is also included about all domestic varieties of cats.

But this book serves another public also, that of schools, technical colleges and students taking elementary biology courses at the universities. The trend in modern biological teaching is to make the courses more practical and relevant to everyday affairs. The basic principles of genetics are usually introduced to students by way of Mendel's peas: tall, short, wrinkled, smooth, etc. A study of coat pattern in mice is also often used, but tends to be elaborate. A simple start can be made in a much more acceptable manner by considering cats whose differences in colour pattern and conformation are well known and easily appreciated, and their inheritance, though at first sight complex, can easily be understood. The greater human appeal of cats is also a help and this is further enhanced in the book by constant reference to features seen in photographs of named pedigree cats. Studies of patterns of behaviour in animals are taking a firm place in both universities and schools. The following pages give an introduction to this subject too. Biologists may also appreciate the data included upon man-made and naturally occurring varieties. And many may find the short history of a planned scientific project both interesting and an indication of the mode of utilization of scientific knowledge.

7

My thanks are due: to Mrs I. Hancox, Mrs B. Nicholas and Mrs R. Levy for their kindness in reading the manuscript and making helpful suggestions; to my husband, Dr J. P. Harding for his unfailing interest in my cats and for the patience and time he has expended upon their photography; and to Mr John Adriaan for kindly allowing two of his photographs to be reproduced as Photographs 31 and 32, and to Mrs H. Noddin for supplying Photographs 21a and b of Mingchiu Murdock.

S. M. Manton (Mrs J. P. Harding),
Mingchiu Cattery,
88 Ennerdale Road,
Richmond, Surrey,
England.

Contents

Illustrations

Colour Illustrations

1. Introduction

What is a Colourpoint? Some twenty years of planned and selective breeding in England had by 1968 produced the superb show type Persian or Longhair cat with the Siamese colour pattern, which has taken high honours on the show benches of the world (Colour photographs I-V). This comparatively new variety of cat, first given official recognition by the Governing Council of the Cat Fancy of Britain in 1955, is now widely recognized as one of the most worthwhile and delightful of pets.

In California, some three years after the breeding of Colourpoints was seriously started in England, the first Himalayans were in the making. These two varieties are roughly the same in general appearance. The objective in England is to produce a Colourpoint Longhair or Persian cat (the words carry the same meaning), with the good type found in other colour varieties of Longhair, which means breeding cats which are say 99.9 per cent Persian or Longhair in their genetical makeup and carry, from the Siamese forbear, only the genes controlling coat pattern. Among breeders of the United States there is considerable difference of opinion as to what is the aim of Himalayan breeding and how it should be achieved. The facts of animal breeding and the genetical basis of colour and of body conformation in cats is not, and can never be, influenced by opinionated Cat Fancy legislation; it is desirable that the genetical basis of Siamese, Persian and Himalayans be understood and it is essential that legislation be moulded upon the facts, not upon opinions.

Meanwhile a clear understanding of the aims and genetics of Colourpoint breeding in England has enabled steady progress to be made, unhampered by ill-conceived legislation. And the result is seen in the performance of English Colourpoints on the show benches of all countries where they compete successfully not only with Himalayans but with other varieties of Longhair. This success is not due to the three years' start enjoyed by Colourpoints over Himalayans, but to the manner of breeding of the former, as is shown in the following pages. The data presented here are based upon the work that has been achieved in the Briarry and Mingchiu catteries in England. The cats will be referred to by their English name of Colourpoint, an abbreviation of Colourpoint Longhair. Confusion in terminology is occasioned by the existence of the category Colourpoint Shorthair in America, comprising cats which in England are called Red-pointed Siamese. The scientific data which are summarized below are equally applicable to American Himalayans.

The following pages have been compiled for breeders and owners of Colourpoints (or Himalayans) who have made no special study of cytology and genetics, but wish to understand the origin of Colourpoints and their breeding and improvement. And it must be emphasized that these cats have captivated the world not only by their beauty, but by their unique and delightful temperament which, when they are permitted a free domestic existence without pens, delights their owners.

The beginnings of Colourpoints, from the chance matings of cats with no known owners, if they had owners, to a simple cross such as that between a Longhair Blue (Photograph 14) and a Seal-point Siamese (a Chocolate-point is shown in Photograph 33), were humble. The Briarry cattery in Richmond, England, owned by the late Mr B. A. Stirling-Webb, was the home of most of the budding Colourpoints. Unknown to him at that time, the development of the American Himalayan was started by the late Mrs Goforth, and only three years after the beginning of his serious enterprise, one which occupied him until the end of his life.

For nearly ten years the Mingchiu cattery joined forces with the Briarry cattery in the progressive breeding of Colourpoints, there being then only a few other breeders of Colourpoints in England. It is the Mingchiu cattery which has developed the finest-typed show specimens, together with two new colour varieties, the Lilac and Chocolate-pointed Colourpoints, and at the same time two other new varieties the Self-chocolate Longhair and Self-lilac Longhair. The Self-chocolate Longhair was first created by Mr Stirling-Webb. Today there is a growing number of enthusiastic breeders of Colourpoints located in very many parts of England, Wales and Scotland, and Colourpoints from this country have passed to most European countries for breeding and have been exported to all the continents of the world. Present-day air travel makes it easier to send a kitten from London to Western Canada or Honolulu than it is to send a kitten to many parts of the British Isles! A breeding pair of Colourpoints frequently starts the propagation of this delightful cat in regions where none had previously existed and where there is little information about them.

Domestic varieties of cat differ in the general shape of the body, in the type of coat and in the colouring of the hair and eyes. In Britain three groups of domestic varieties have been recognized by the Governing Council of the Cat Fancy, but the distinctions between them are not absolute, intermediates exist, and some of the newer varieties do not fit into any of the three categories. The system is due for revision, but until this is made the present classification stands. The group of varieties known as 'Longhair' has the same meaning as the older terms 'Persian' and 'Angora'; they are cats possessing all features of body conformation found in good type Persians of other countries. The Longhair varieties contrast in coat length with the Shorthair varieties. In Britain the latter are subdivided into the 'British' and the 'Foreign' types, an unfortunate insular method of description, because all varieties of domestic cats are international.

The Longhair varieties of cat are characterized by a massive 'cobby' body, a compact and powerfully built frame, with short legs, wide feet and short tail (Colour photographs V, VIII, XI, Photographs 5, 17, 18). The head is round with good cranial width, the ears small, tufted and outwardly directed, the nose short and well turned off the forehead and the face wide with large round eyes (Colour photographs I, III, IV, Photographs 1, 11, 14). The coat is long, the hair silky for choice, rather than woolly, and in winter a long frill frames the face, the tail carrying a full brush the width of the body (Colour photographs I, III, VII, Photographs 2, 3, 13). Typical varieties of Longhair are: Orange-eyed Black (Photographs 16, 20); Orange and Blue-eyed Whites; Blue (Photograph 14); Cream; Blue-Cream; Tortoiseshell; Tortoiseshell and White; Chinchilla; Silver, Brown and Red Tabbies; Red Self; Smoke; Colourpoint; and Bicoloured. The Birman and the Turkish Cat differ in some respects from typical Longhairs; the Balinese as yet unrecognized by the G.C.C.F., does not fit in here at all in spite of its long coat.

15

The Shorthair varieties carry a short coat, not of the same kind in all, and two main conformations of body. In general, the further east in distribution the longer is the face and the more wedge-shaped the head, with large ears. The further west in distribution the broader is the head and face and the smaller the ears. The 'British' cats tend towards the western type and the 'Foreign' cats towards the eastern type. The 'British' Shorthair type possesses a round head, short nose and tail, powerful body, round ears, etc. (Photograph 15), in contrast to the 'Foreign' Shorthair with long, lithe, lightly built bodies, longer and more wedge-shaped heads, ears large, tall and pointed, tail long and tapering, paws narrow and dainty, etc. (Photograph 33). Typical 'British' varieties are: the Orange-eyed Black (Photograph 15); Blue and Orange-eyed Whites; Blue; Cream; Blue-cream; Tortoiseshell; Tortoiseshell and White; Silver, Brown and Red Tabbies; Bicoloured; and Spotted. Typical 'Foreign' Shorthair varieties are: Siamese (Photograph 33); Burmese; Foreign White (a dominant white variety of the Siamese type); Abyssinian; and Chestnut Brown. The adopted standard for the 'Russian Blue' differs somewhat from the above. The Devon and Cornish Rex cats have coats lacking the long guard hairs, leaving the soft undercoat which tends to be wavy.

A third conformation of body, but not recognized by the G.C.C.F., as distinct from 'British Shorthair', is the Manx, a tailless cat which borders on the abnormal. All conditions exist between the entire absence of a tail and partial tails in kittens from Manx parents. The Longhair genetical factor can also occur in Manx, as in many other varieties.

The agouti grey fur of many wild species of mammals is composed of hairs which are individually ticked (striped). Three basic colours make up the grey coat, the black, chocolate (brown) and yellow pigments. The paler grey areas on a Tabby cat are made up of ticked fur. The pattern on a Tabby is formed by hairs in which the colour tends towards solid black. In a Red Tabby the yellow (or red) pigment almost replaces the black, and ticking, but not the striping, is almost eliminated. Ticking is also found in the coats of the Chinchilla, Abyssinian, Smoke and Manx. There is no ticking in the coats of Black, Blue, Blue-cream, Tortoiseshell, Tortie and White, or in the Seal, Blue, Chocolate and Lilac-pointed cats. The Red Tabby and

I THE FINEST COLOURPOINT OF 1969
Ch. Mingchiu Mudoba, Seal-pointed male, aged 14 months. He possesses deep blue eyes combined with a short, well-demarcated nose, other features of good type and a long, dense, outstanding coat.

Red Self are genetically similar in essentials. Cream is a dilute form of Red; and the basic genotype of the Chinchilla is akin to that of the Silver Tabby.

In Siamese, Birmans and Colourpoints there is a reduction of pigment, and it is largely restricted to the extremities, the nose, ears, feet and tail, which are called the points. A basic colour is Seal-point, and this is modified by additional genetical factors to produce Blue, Chocolate and Lilac-points, with some corresponding changes in the body colour. Seal brown corresponds with Black among self-coloured cats; the Blue and Lilac-points correspond with the similarly named Self-coloured varieties, and the Chocolate-point corresponds with the 'Chestnut Brown', 'Foreign', 'Havana' and Brown Burmese. Red points do not belong to this series, and ticking is scarcely present outside the solid colour of the ghost stripes which appear on the points. Tortoiseshell, Tabby and other coloured points have been bred in the Siamese, but to a lesser extent in the Longhairs.

Many other varieties of cat can be produced which breed true. Some of these have been made by planned breeding in the United States of America, but they have as yet not gained recognition from the Governing Council of the Cat Fancy in Britain.

It is suggested that readers without specialized knowledge of cytology should take for granted the detailed and well established evidence for the facts to which reference is made in Chapters 2 and 3 regarding the equal chances of eggs being fertilized by different types of sperms. These matters rest upon sound foundations which need not be fully comprehended for the rest of the account to be intelligible to anyone interested in the subject. There are popular books in plenty which deal with inheritance, but in such a superficial manner, toned down for consumption by the uninitiated, as to be quite useless for all practical purposes of the cat breeder, or of the interested owner of a Colourpoint or a Himalayan.

Most of the varieties of cat which have been used in the development of Colourpoints are shown in the photographs reproduced on the plates. An attempt has been made to illustrate pictorially the stages in the advancement of the variety in its several colours. No cats are particularly co-operative towards a photographer. Some view the necessary lights with a scowl or an expression of disgust upon their faces, others flatly refuse to sit for their portraits. Kittens greet the situation with cross or glum resignation or with escape. Some cats, such as Ch. Mingchiu Monique and Ch. Mingchiu Chou-Lu (Photographs 13, 22) always prick their ears to the bright lights, so spoiling their heads, photographically, and masking their good type. The photographs shown almost entirely depict cats from the Mingchiu cattery because of their accessibility and because it is here that most progress has been made in recent years in the advancement of Colourpoints and in the creation of other varieties.

2. The reproductive cycle and breeding pairs

The body of the cat is made up of multitudes of microscopic units called cells, each of which contains the bearers of the many determinants of hereditary characters. The bearers, termed the chromosomes, occur in pairs and each member of a pair is like its fellow. A pair of these bearers can be represented thus: ( ) ( ). But in the eggs and sperms produced by the cat these bearers are single, thus: ( ). Take a pair of cats, male and female: they will produce eggs, one thousandth of an inch in size, whose bearers can be represented as ( ), and sperms, much smaller in size, each containing one bearer ( ) or chromosome from every original pair.

After the mating of the female by the male, each egg produced is fertilized by one sperm, the two fusing together. The fertilized egg can be represented as ( ) ( ), the double number of bearers being restored by the fusion of the egg and sperm.

The bearers of hereditary characters, the chromosomes, in an animal cell are few in number, 18 pairs and the sex chromosomes in cats, and each carries a large number of 'genes', each gene being the determinant of some characteristic of the animal. Simple examples are given below which show the inheritance and segregation of genes borne on different bearers or chromosomes. The number of hereditary characters in an animal, and therefore the number of genes, is very great, far greater than the number of chromosomes, thus one chromosome carries many genes.

When the genes for two different characters are borne by the same chromosome, the genes tend to be inherited together, and do not show the 'segregation' taking place at the formation of eggs and sperm, and at fertilization, which is described below. 'Linkage' and 'partial linkage' are more complex phenomena than those appertaining to the inheritance of the major characteristics of Colourpoints, and they are not necessary for understanding the account given of Seal, Blue, Chocolate and Lilac-pointed Colourpoints. However, it is possible to breed other coloured points in the Longhairs, such as Tortoiseshell and Red, and here an understanding of sex-linked inheritance is needed and is described in Chapter 8. These two colour varieties have been produced mainly in America; their genetics is parallel to that of the Red and Tortoiseshell-points of Siamese.

Cats for breeding should be the finest specimens which the breeder can obtain. And this means well grown and healthy as well as of good appearance, the cats being worthy representatives of their variety. The difference in prices of kittens is determined by their show-bench potential, other factors being equal. The finest kittens are not easy to come by or to breed, and are much sought after. The range of price in kittens is a small sum compared with the upkeep for life, 13–20 years or so, and if breeding is the object, economy in purchase price is pointless. The difficulty at the present time is to secure top flyers, unless you breed them yourself.

Pairs of Colourpoints for breeding should be selected from different parentage. But a male and female, sired by the same outstanding cat, is permissible when the other parent of each represents a distinctly different line of breeding. Brother to sister and parent to offspring matings are usually best avoided. Both parents are equally important in transmitting the heritable characters to their kittens. But if the parents are closely related there is a chance of both of them transmitting the same lethal or undesirable genes to the kittens. Such genes in single dose are harmless, but in double dose (homozygous) they exercise their deleterious or lethal effects.

Since no Colourpoints are yet perfect, the variety being in the process of evolution, it is desirable either to make up breeding pairs from the most outstanding specimens available, or to form a pair in which the shortcomings of the one are countered by the strong points of the other, the requirements mentioned above also being met. For example: do not breed from a pair of cats both possessing too long or too straight a nose (Colour photograph X, Photograph 32), too narrow a top of head with large upright ears wide open at the base (Photographs 34, 35), too little colour in the eye, too long in the body and tail, or with poor coat. Kittens from such pairs are not likely to be very good looking, however healthy and well brought up they may be. The breeding of delightful pet type kittens is not a saving in expense, and does not help the progress of the variety. The chances of breeding an outstanding kitten is far greater from a balanced pair of cats, there will be a range in type among their kittens and some may be a substantial improvement on either parent and others can be expected to be the reverse. The manner of building up good type in Colourpoints is considered in Chapter 4.

3. Inheritance and segregation of paired characteristics

Visible characteristics are often inherited as pairs of opposites, for example in the cat, *Longhair* versus *Shorthair*. (This example is not ideally simple because intermediate lengths of coat exist, and we know that this pair of opposites is really composite, hair length being controlled not by one but by a number of paired 'genes'.) But some understanding of the inheritance of long and of short hair is a first essential, because the genes controlling the Siamese colour pattern were introduced into the Longhairs from Shorthairs.

One character of each pair is usually dominant to the other (there are cases of incomplete dominance, but they need not be considered now, see p. 70). Short hair is *dominant* to long, that is a cat carrying the genes for both is always short haired. The *recessive* characteristic, long hair, is only visual in cats genetically 'pure' for this character and carrying no gene for short hair. This is made clear by the following matings.

EXAMPLE 1

Let us cross a LONGHAIRED FEMALE (Colour photograph XII, Photographs 12, 14) with a SHORTHAIRED MALE (Photograph 33). Let the Longhair genes be LL and the Shorthair genes be SS in these cats.

The eggs will all be: The sperms will all be:

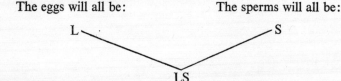

L   S

LS

The fertilized eggs and the resulting kittens (first filial or F 1 generation) will be LS in composition.

The S gene is dominant to the L gene, so the F 1 kittens will all be Shorthair (Photographs 15, 31) but invisibly carrying the gene for

Longhair, heterozygous for Longhair and Shorthair, i.e. one gene of each and not two as in the homozygous parents.

If we now mate together two such Shorthair cats, each carrying the Longhair gene:

SHORTHAIR CARRYING LONGHAIR	SHORTHAIR CARRYING LONGHAIR
FEMALE	MALE
SL	SL
the eggs will be	the sperms will be
of two kinds:	of two kinds:
S	S
L	L

Egg S has an equal chance of being fertilized by sperm S or by sperm

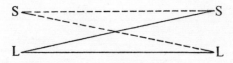

L, giving fertilized eggs and F 2 kittens SS and SL, see dotted lines above. Egg L has an equal chance of being fertilized by Sperm S or by sperm L, see solid lines above, giving fertilized eggs and kittens LS and LL. Thus in all there will be in the F 2 generation of kittens:

LL	LS SL[1]	SS
One pure Longhair cat, which will breed nothing but Longhair when mated to the same. (in appearance as in Photograph 20)	Two Shorthair cats carrying Longhair invisibly, and which can breed exactly like the F 1 cats. (e.g. Photograph 15)	One pure Shorthair cat which carries no Longhair and will produce nothing but Shorthair when mated to the same.

These proportions 1:2:1 will be the average expectation from a

[1]LS and SL are genetically identical.

23

large number of litters. One litter may deviate considerably from the average.

It should be noted that the SS cats and the SL cats look alike, all Shorthair (Photograph 15), and can only be differentiated by further breeding, so from the above mating the expectation is one Longhair to three Shorthair.

EXAMPLE 2

Now take another simple pair of characters (called an allelomorphic pair), that of a SELF OR SOLID-COLOURED cat (Black, Blue, Brown, etc.) and one with the SIAMESE COLOUR PATTERN (Photograph 33). Let us mate a Solid-coloured cat, Black for example, with a Siamese. The solid colour is dominant to the patterned coat.

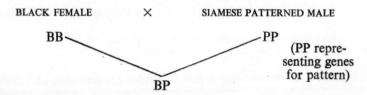

BLACK FEMALE   ×   SIAMESE PATTERNED MALE

BB   PP

(PP representing genes for pattern)

BP

As in Example 1 above, the F 1 cats produced by such a mating will all be BP in composition and will all appear black (Photograph 15) but will carry the Siamese coat pattern[1].

Next, mate together two such Black carriers

BP   ×   BP

There will be two kinds of eggs B and P and two kinds of sperms B and P, and each egg has an equal chance of being fertilized by either type of sperm, as in Example 1.

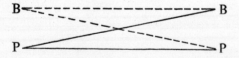

B   B

P   P

[1]Other colours may appear in the F 1 generation if the Black and Siamese parents each carry similar genes for recessive characters, such as blue.

1a

1b

A MATURING MALE

Above: Champion Mingchiu Polo, Seal-pointed male, sired by a Self-blue carrier, Briarry Valparago. At 9 months he shows the typical incomplete mask of the adolescent. *Below:* Polo at $5\frac{1}{2}$ years, showing spread of the mask and fine set of the ears, wide top of head, short nose, etc. He has sired many champions.

2

THE FULL PALE COAT, DARK SEAL POINTS AND FINE TYPE
Above: Ch. Briarry Candytuft at 8 months. She left no progeny. *Right:* Ch. Mingchiu Chou-Lu at $8\frac{1}{2}$ months, ears momentarily pricked, short nose, firm chin, fine coat, and later an efficient stud.

Compare with Photographs 8, 9 opposite p. 40.

Top: 3-month-old Seal-points of 1954, ears too upright, tops of head too narrow, noses too long.

Centre: 3-month-old Seal-point of 1957, ears well set, nose short, the body is cobby, tail is short, Ch. Mingchiu Chou-Lu (cf. Photographs 13, 17, 18).

Below, left: 7-month-old Seal-pointed female of 1968 with fine type, Ch. Mingchiu Obel, adult in Colour Photograph IV. Her ancestry has 6 out-crosses to Self-coloured Long-hairs. *Right:* 6-month-old Blue-point male Mingchiu Roy, with 4 outcrosses to Self-coloured Longhairs in his ancestry.

so giving the F2 generation of kittens of the following composition:

BB	BP BP	PP
One pure Black cat, which will breed nothing but Black when mated to the same.	Two Black cats carrying the Siamese pattern, and can breed like the F1 above.	One pure Siamese, which will breed nothing but Siamese when mated to the same.

These will appear as three Blacks and one Siamese out of four, on the average.

Note particularly in both these examples that the recessive characters, Longhair in Example 1 and Siamese pattern in Example 2, if visible at all, are pure. The dominant characters, Shorthair and Black, on the contrary may be pure (homozygous, in double dose) or in the heterozygous state may mask a recessive gene which is being carried.

EXAMPLE 3

Now let us take the inheritance of two 'allelomorphic' pairs of characters together, and as an example, let us make a COLOURPOINT from a LONGHAIR BLACK cat (Photograph 20 in appearance) and a SHORTHAIR SIAMESE (Photograph 33), that is combining the examples given separately above. This can be done in two or more generations.

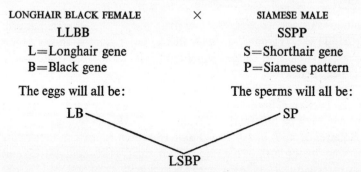

LONGHAIR BLACK FEMALE × SIAMESE MALE

LLBB   SSPP

L=Longhair gene   S=Shorthair gene
B=Black gene   P=Siamese pattern

The eggs will all be: The sperms will all be:

LB   SP

LSBP

so that the fertilized eggs and the F1 kittens will all be LSBP in composition and Shorthaired and Black in appearance, the dominant characters, but all will carry the recessive genes for Longhair and Siamese pattern (Photograph 15).

25

From the F 1 cats bred together,

LSBP	×	LSBP
there will be four		there will be four
kind of eggs:		kinds of sperms:
LB		LB
LP		LP
SB		SB
SP		SP

As before, each egg has an equal chance of being fertilized by any type of sperm. The results of such fertilizations, 16 in number, are most easily expressed by a table as shown. An egg of type LB can be fertilized by sperm LB, see Square 1. An egg of type LB can be fertilized by sperm LP, see Square 2. An egg of type LP can be fertilized by sperm SP, see Square 8, and so on.

Each square represents the composition of an F 2 kitten. The variety represents the average expectation among sixteen kittens resulting from the F 1 × F 1 type of matings, but much larger numbers of kittens may be required to give this average.

It will be noted that only four of these cats will be genetically 'pure' for the characters under consideration. Square 1 shows a pure Longhair Black, homozygous for both Longhair and Black, and therefore carrying none of the opposite genes. Square 6 shows a pure Colourpoint, homozygous for Longhair and for the Siamese pattern. Square 11 shows a pure Shorthair Black, and Square 16 shows a pure Siamese. These four cats when mated to the same will produce only cats like themselves.

Squares 2 and 5 show Longhair Black cats carrying the Siamese colour pattern (Photograph 20), they look like the cat in Square 1, and can only be differentiated from it by further breeding.

Squares 3, 4, 7, 9, 10, 12, 13 and 15 are all Shorthair Black cats carrying one or both of the recessive characters (Photograph 15) and they externally resemble the pure Shorthair Black in Square 11, from which they can only be differentiated by further breeding. Squares 14 and 8 show Siamese cats carrying Longhair (Photograph 31), and they are visibly indistinguishable from the pure Siamese in Square 16.

Note that only one of the sixteen cats shows its certain genetical

Types of eggs	Types of sperms			
	LB	LP	SB	SP
LB	1 LLBB ★ pure Longhair Black	2 LLBP ★ Longhair Black carrying Siamese pattern Photograph 29	3 LSBB ● Shorthair Black carrying Longhair	4 LSBP ● Shorthair Black carrying Longhair and Siamese pattern Photograph 15
LP	5 LLBP ★ Longhair Black carrying Siamese pattern	6 LLPP **Longhair with Siamese pattern, COLOUR-POINT pure** Photograph 12	7 LSPB ● Shorthair Black carrying Longhair and Siamese pattern	8 LSPP O Shorthair Siamese pattern carrying Longhair
SB	9 LSBB ● Shorthair Black carrying Longhair	10 LSBP ● Shorthair Black carrying Longhair and Siamese pattern	11 SSBB ● pure Shorthair Black	12 SSBP ● Shorthair Black carrying Siamese pattern
SP	13 LSBP ● Shorthair Black carrying Longhair and Siamese pattern	14 LSPP O Shorthair Siamese pattern carrying Longhair Photograph 31	15 SSBP ● Shorthair Black carrying Siamese pattern	16 SSPP O Shorthair Siamese pure for both Shorthair and coat pattern Photograph 33

The marks ★, O and ● in the top right of the squares denote cats of the same external appearance.

composition by its appearance, the Colourpoint in Square 6 (Photograph 12). And this is because both the characteristics of this variety of cat, the Longhair and the Siamese pattern are recessive, and therefore if they are visible at all, the cat must be pure for each. The Colourpoint, when you get it, breeds true when mated to the same:

27

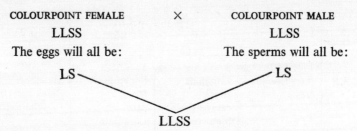

COLOURPOINT FEMALE $\times$ COLOURPOINT MALE

LLSS   LLSS

The eggs will all be: The sperms will all be:

LS   LS

LLSS

so that the ensuing fertilized eggs and kittens will all be LLSS in composition and just like the parents in appearance. No number of extra generations of Colourpoints will make them more pure, genetically, than they are when they first appear. The Colourpoint is formed by the segregation and recombination of very well known genes, or determinants of hereditary characters, and this can occur in the wild as well as under human control. There is nothing particularly man made about any of the steps by which a Colourpoint is produced.

Colourpoints can also be bred from many other cats in the table above. Any of the Longhair Blacks carrying the Siamese colour pattern, Squares 2 and 5, with genetical composition LLBP, when mated together will produce a Colourpoint:,

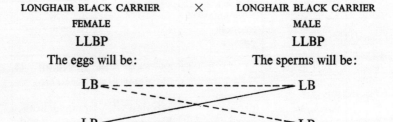

LONGHAIR BLACK CARRIER $\times$ LONGHAIR BLACK CARRIER

FEMALE   MALE

LLBP   LLBP

The eggs will be: The sperms will be:

LB   LB

LP   LP

Fertilization of these eggs by the sperms to produce the F 3 generation will give fertilized eggs and kittens:

LLBB	LLBP LLBP	LLPP
One pure Longhair Black	Two Longhair Blacks carrying the Siamese pattern	One pure Colourpoint, Longhair with Siamese pattern

Thus one out of four cats in this F 3 generation will be Colourpoint.

28

Similarly the Longhair Black carrier in Square 2 mated to a Shorthair Black carrying both Longhair and Siamese pattern in Square 4, will produce one Colourpoint in eight in the F3 generation.

The Siamese cats carrying Longhair in Squares 8 and 14 also can produce a Colourpoint when mated together and in the proportion of one in four.

A number of matings of cats in the table will not produce Colourpoints. The pure Longhair Black, Shorthair Black and Siamese in Squares 1, 11 and 16 will only produce the same when each type is mated to the same. The Shorthair Blacks in Squares 3 and 9 when mated together will produce no Colourpoint because they carry no Siamese pattern. The Shorthair Blacks in Squares 12 and 15 mated together will also produce no Colourpoint because they carry no Longhair. But a Shorthair Black in Square 4 mated to a Shorthair Black in Square 10 will produce one Colourpoint in sixteen.

If now a Colourpoint is mated to a Longhair carrier of the Siamese coat pattern:

COLOURPOINT FEMALE	×	LONGHAIR BLACK CARRIER OF SIAMESE PATTERN MALE (Photograph 20)
LLPP		LLBP
The eggs will all be:		The sperms will be:

LP ⟨ LB
LP

giving fertilized eggs and kittens:

LLBP	LLPP
Black Longhair carriers of the Siamese pattern	Colourpoints

Thus the use of one Colourpoint parent increases the expectation of Colourpoints in the progeny to half of the offspring.

Since it is impossible to tell by the external appearance whether, say, a Longhair Black carries Colourpoint or not, there are obvious

29

practical difficulties to the breeder. But such a cat descended from one Colourpoint parent, or which produces at any time one Colourpoint offspring, is then known to be a carrier.

The matings just described can all occur naturally without the intervention of Man wherever Longhair cats and Siamese have opportunity for mating. That Colourpoints do not turn up so very often in this way is understandable since the chances are only 1:16 when two carriers meet for the F2 generation. But the chances of a Colourpoint turning up without human direction increases with time and additional generations of carriers, as shown above. Colourpoints have in fact turned up in several parts of the world where Siamese and Longhair cats coexist. They have been found in Scotland, Cornwall, Devon, Kenya and probably lots of other places, and the first Colourpoint owned by Mr Stirling-Webb was a stray found in a churchyard. No owner could be found. Had such a cat been purposely bred it would surely have been of great value to the owner as being the first of its kind in this country. There is no difference whatever in the natural occurrence of Colourpoints and in those produced by controlled matings, as far as the basic nature of the cats is concerned. But the chances of finding a Colourpoint of type so good as to be worthy of a championship is as unlikely as the finding of a champion type Chinchilla in the wild.

4. Type and eye colour in Colourpoints and their inheritance

Having produced a Colourpoint purposely, or having found one that has turned up by accidental matings, the 'type' of these cats does not come up to the standard expected by the Governing Council of the Cat Fancy in Britain today. The nose is too long and straight (Colour photograph X), the face too narrow (Photograph 35), the ears too large and set too much on top of the head (Photographs 4, 34), the legs and tail are too long, the paws too dainty and the coat too short (cf. Colour photographs I–VII, Photographs 1–3, 11–13, 17, 18).

There are various ways in which the type can be improved, that is altered towards the Persian or Longhair type, with short, well-demarcated nose, round head, wide face, small, outwardly directed ears, 'cobby' body and short legs and tail, with large feet and a very full coat up to five inches or so in length (Colour photographs I–VIII, Photographs 8, 9, 13, 17, 18, 19, 21), which is the aim of progressive Colourpoint breeding in England. The object of such breeding is to produce a cat similar in type to the finest Persian or Longhair (Photograph 14), but exhibiting the Siamese colour pattern, in other words a colour variety of the Persian or Longhair cat (Colour photograph V).

Within the same litter of Colourpoint kittens there may be considerable individual variation, or there may not, even when the parents are very similar. Much work has been done on the variation which occurs within a 'pure line' of animals and plants, and for this it has been useful to take characters which can be measured precisely, such as height or weight.

Within one pure line the number of individuals in the population which show the extremes, in say height or weight, is small compared with the much larger number which approach the average in these features. The distribution of these characters among the population of one pure line is shown by Graph A.

(A)

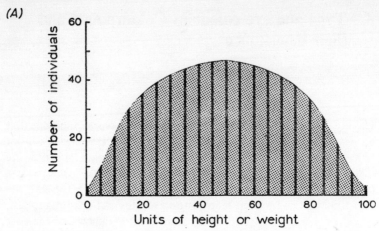

Normal distribution of height or weight in the population of one pure line.

If now we breed from individuals chosen from the extreme ends of such a range, using, say, the tallest or the heaviest individuals for mating, and repeat the process, selecting at each generation for the most extreme individuals for further breeding. The distribution of height or weight within the ensuing population can be graphically represented as before (Graph B).

(B)

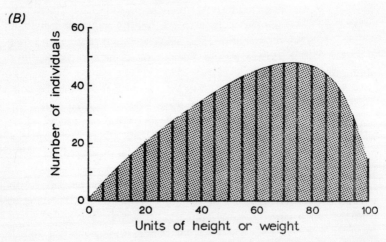

The effect of selective breeding for extreme height or weight in one pure line.

II THE CREAM OF BRITISH COLOURPOINTS IN 1969

Above: Ch. Mingchiu Tinka in her first adolescent winter coat, the winning female at the National Cat Club show in London, December 1967.

III *Below*: Ch. Mingchiu Chirk, a Blue-point male with wide short nose, wide top of head, well-set ears and good frill framing the face. He carries Chocolate and sires kittens with bluer eyes than his and with Seal, Blue, Chocolate or Lilac points.

The peak showing the largest number of similar individuals lies nearer to the original extreme, but the range does not go beyond it. In other words, selection within a pure line has not really produced anything new but has only altered the proportion of individuals of the different weights or heights, within the community.

Now what is the bearing of this on the breeding of Colourpoints? With the object of improving the type, Colourpoint has been bred to Colourpoint, for a number of generations, selecting from each batch of kittens the better looking ones for further breeding. The results of many years of selective breeding along these lines is seen in the average Himalayan cat of America today, which cannot compete successfully with the best British Colourpoints bred along different lines. The type produced by the selective method is inferior to that which can be produced in the same amount of breeding time but along the lines described below. The simple examples of variation within pure lines given above are not exactly applicable to the much more complex genetical composition of Colourpoints, but the broad principles are somewhat the same. It is not at all surprising that selective breeding from Colourpoint to Colourpoint matings has produced no greater strides in improvement in type over a few years. It is true that in certain varieties of cat spectacular changes appear to have resulted from selection, alone, but over very many years. The Chinchilla appears to have the same basic genetical make up as the Silver Tabby, and may have arisen by selection therefrom (Robinson, 1959[1]). Our fashionable and very long nosed Siamese, which are not admired by all, are the result of selection on the part of breeders and judges. The selection making this trend has already been overdone (Hindley, 1967)[2] and the lower jaw has usually not kept pace with the elongation of the face above it.

The more productive way of improving type in Colourpoints is by outcrossing to the best type Persian cat that can be obtained, say a Black or Blue Longhair (Photograph 14 and see below). At this point it becomes desirable to relinquish the symbols L, S, B and P used above for the sake of simplicity, and turn to those which represent the genetical make up of various varieties of cats more precisely and

[1]Robinson, R., 1959, 'Genetics of the domestic cat', *Bibliogr. Genet.* **18**, 273–362, 3 figs, 15 tabs.
[2]Hindley, G., 1967, *Siamese Cats, Past and Present*, London.

in more detail. The symbols adopted from here onwards are those in common use, for example by Robinson and by Searle.[1] A Shorthair Black can be represented by aa, a Longhair Black by an additional pair of genes ll, the genetical composition of this cat becoming $aa\,ll$ for the factors under consideration.[2] A Colourpoint is represented by $aa\,ll\,c^s c^s$, the last two symbols representing the genes determining the Siamese coat pattern.

Let us mate together:

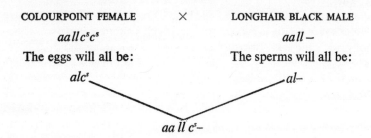

COLOURPOINT FEMALE	×	LONGHAIR BLACK MALE
$aa\,ll\,c^s c^s$		$aa\,ll\,-$
The eggs will all be:		The sperms will all be:
$al\,c^s$		$al\,-$

$$aa\,ll\,c^s -$$

The fertilized eggs will be $aa\,ll\,c^s -$ in composition, there being no fellow for the gene c^s, its absence being indicated by the –. The F 1 kittens will all be Longhair Blacks carrying the Siamese colour pattern (Photograph 16).

It so happens that the carriers are often much finer in type than the Colourpoint parent, although some are no better. A few are as fine as any other Persian of the same variety, e.g. Ch. Mingchiu Magog (Photograph 20), a Black Longhair carrier, who has been unbeaten on the show bench by any other Black, either as a kitten or as an adult. Such carriers are invaluable for Colourpoint breeding, but must not be used to excess, or too much eye colour is lost (see below).

[1]Robinson, R., 1959, 'Genetics of the domestic cat', *Bibliogr. Genet.* **18**, 273–362, 3 figs, 15 tabs.
Searle, A. G., 1968, *Comparative Genetics of Coat Colour in Mammals*, Logos Press Academic Press i–xii. 1–308.

[2]It should be noted that the genes BB on the preceding pages stand for solid or self colour, Black being taken as an example. The basic colour Black in the Longhair and Shorthair varieties is probably determined by several pairs of genes which need not be considered here. The gene symbol aa means the recessive Non-agouti determinant, which converts the wild Tabby type to Black.

Next, let us mate together:

COLOURPOINT MALE	×	LONGHAIR BLACK CARRIER
(e.g. Ch. Mingchiu Polo		FEMALE
Photograph 1b)		(e.g. Woods Amber)
$aallc^sc^s$		$aallc^s-$

The sperms will all be: The eggs will be of two kinds:

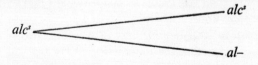

$$alc^s \diagup \begin{array}{c} alc^s \\ al- \end{array}$$

giving fertilized eggs and kittens: $aallc^sc^s$ and $aallc^s-$ which are respectively Colourpoint and Black Longhairs carrying Colourpoint, in equal numbers on the average. The type of these Colourpoints varies from one to another, but some are a substantial improvement on the Colourpoint parent, but again on the average, and not necessarily so in every litter.

Eleven litters actually obtained:

(1) 2 Colourpoints, 2 Blacks
  (Photograph 16)
(2) 2 Blacks
(3) 2 Blacks, 1 Blue
(4) 1 Colourpoint, 1 Blue
(5) 2 Colourpoints
(6) 2 Colourpoints
(7) 3 Colourpoints, 1 Black
(8) 2 Colourpoints
(9) 1 Blue, 1 Black
(10) 3 Colourpoints, 1 Black
(11) 5 Colourpoints

The greater number of our finest Colourpoints have been produced thus from one parental Self-coloured carrier, either a Blue or a Black (Photograph 20). Mr B. A. Stirling-Webb's well-known Colourpoint stud, Ch. Briarry Euan, was produced from the mating of two carriers, a Longhair Black and a Longhair Blue, hence his excellence in type. Ch. Mingchiu Tinka (Colour photograph II), the winning Colourpoint female at the National Show, London, 1967, where some forty Colourpoints were exhibited, was bred from a Black Longhair dam and sired by a Colourpoint. Gr. Ch. Mingchiu Pearlas of Harobed, for three seasons winner of 'All Eastern Himalayan and American Honorable Mention Blue-point' is out of a Colourpoint dam by a Blue Longhair carrier, her litter brother being

35

Ch. Mingchiu Polo (Photographs 1, 24). One cannot count on such outstanding kittens as these at every breeding. Between 1963 when Polo and Pearlas were born and 1967 when Chou-lu (Photographs 13, 17, 18) was born to the same dam, I had no other such outstanding kitten from her when she was bred to a number of different studs. The Blue Longhair carrier, Briarry Valparago, belonging to Mr Stirling-Webb and sire of Polo and Pearlas, was dead, and not until Ch. Mingchiu Shan was grown to maturity did I find a suitable mate for this female, Briarry Jehane.

The reason for the improvement in type obtained in the manner described above is that the outcrossing to the Self-coloured Longhair or Persian brings in many more of the genes, not considered above, which control the finer characteristics of body conformation and coat which cannot be obtained, or may be obtained only very slowly, by endless mating of Colourpoint to Colourpoint. Such genes can be introduced from outside. Selection must also be exercised on the Self-coloured carriers, and only those of finest type should be used for further breeding.

It has been stated in *Cats* magazine, May 1968, that because the Himalayan was originally produced from Persians combined with Siamese, therefore the end product is not any more Persian than Siamese. The fallacy of this statement is easily demonstrated. When a Siamese is mated to a Persian the genetical make up of the kittens is on average 50 per cent Siamese and 50 per cent Persian. If an outcross is made between these kittens and a Persian or Longhair of excellent type, the ensuing kittens will be only 25 per cent Siamese in their make up. At a second outcross of the same nature the Siamese component of the offspring will be 12·5 per cent, at a third outcross this component will be 6·25 per cent, at a fourth outcross 3·175 per cent, etc. It is clear that with a small number of outcrosses, not necessarily consecutive (there can be Colourpoint to Colourpoint matings in between) the Siamese component of Colourpoints becomes very small indeed. It is the aim of the Mingchiu cattery to carry on with Mr Stirling Webb's intention to produce Colourpoints whose genetical make up comprises say 99·9 per cent for Persian or Longhair type and 0·1 per cent for the Siamese colour pattern. All Persian cats carry genes determining colour, there is no such thing as a cat without colour or dominant white genes. Colour or colour pattern is not linked with the genetical attributes of Longhair or Shorthair cats.

Claims have been made in the USA that outcrossing to Persians has produced no improvement in Himalayan type. But intense surprise has been registered there at the unexpected full Persian appearance of Mingchiu Blue and Black carriers! It is useless to outcross to Self-coloured Persians, carriers or otherwise, unless their type is superb, because if this is not so, no progress will result. A superb black carrier is seen in Photograph 20. And the cumulative effect of out-crossing to Self-coloured Longhairs is plainly shown by the photo-graphs (Photographs 6, 7) of Mingchiu Roy and of Ch. Mingchiu Obel as kittens, aged 6 and 7 months respectively, and therefore both at the stage showing relatively large ears; later the body grows to 'fit' the ears (Colour photograph IV). Both kittens have nice type, but that of Obel is decidedly the better, with great face width, short nose, round eyes far apart, etc. Roy's ancestry has four outcrosses to either Self-coloured Longhair (Persians) or Self-coloured carriers and Obel has six such outcrosses in her pedigree. This is the sort of improvement in type which can be obtained in a small span of breed-ing time. Note also the enormous improvement in type from that of the 1960 litter shown in Photograph 35 to the kittens bred nine years later, Photograph 36.

The photographs illustrate very well the change in the conforma-tion of the nose and face resulting from this type of breeding. Long straight noses are seen in Colour photograph X and Photograph 12. A less long nose but with an even curved profile (Photograph 32), at one time characterized many of our Colourpoints, and breeders who mated Colourpoint to Colourpoint claimed that nothing other than this could be achieved. But now the short, wide nose with a good break at the bridge is expected in our best (Colour photographs I, III, IV, Photographs 22, 23). Ch. Mingchiu Ghunti has an out-standingly wide short nose (Colour photograph VII), as is required for a good Longhair or Persian. The whole face is shorter and wider than in the early Colourpoints (cf. Photographs 12 and 13). The chin is firm and does not slope backwards below the upper jaw (Photo-graphs 1, 3, 11, 24).

The ears of many Colourpoints are still too large, even if the top of the head is good, as in Photograph 10, or the ears may be too open at the base (Photograph 34), but they are improving. Kittens with small ears at 2 months (Photograph 8) have relatively large ears by the age of about 4 months (Photographs 4, 5), but thereafter the body grows more rapidly and the ears do not increase (cf. Photograph 6 and Colour photograph IV). Nice small ears, well directed outwards, leaving a wide top to the head are well shown by Ch. Mingchiu Polo (Photographs 1a, b), and the photos of the same cat at various ages illustrate the way in which these features develop in the individual. Well-set good type ears are seen in the kittens in Photographs 5, 6, 7 and in the adult cat in Colour photograph IV; contrast these with Photograph 4, showing kittens with much too large and up-right ears leaving a narrow top to the head. These two kittens looked better when older, but they were not budding champions and they lack the face width seen in Photographs 5, 6, 23. The Black Longhair carriers (Photograph 16), are younger and show very nice short faces, small, well-set ears and good width between the eyes. These charac-teristics are also well illustrated by the very fine Colourpoint kittens in Photographs 8 and 9. The older kitten carries the darker wider mask, but both show the wide face, good ears and top of head, short nose with a good break, firm chin, etc., all of which are the aims of Colourpoint breeding. The kitten in Photograph 2, later a champion, lacked so good a top to the head as seen in Photographs 9 and 18, but she had a most magnificent long coat. By these means the type of Mingchiu Colourpoints today has reached a new level which is decidedly ahead of the results of selection from Colourpoint to Colourpoint matings.

It is no accident that the winning males of the Colourpoint Open class at the National Show have been superseded in four consecutive years by younger and finer ones: Ch. Mingchiu Shan in 1965, Ch. Mingchiu Kamet in 1966, Ch. Mingchiu Chou-Lu in 1967 (Photo-graphs 3, 17, 18) and Ch. Mingchiu Mudoba in 1968 (Colour photo-graphs I, V). But the older boys are not by any means on the shelf, for Shan is the sire of Chou-Lu. No finer demonstration of the effi-cacy of the methods described above, for improvement in type, can be found than in the results of the British 1967–8 show season. Cats from the Mingchiu cattery have taken almost all of the Open classes for adults, '1st and Ch.' for the whole season, sixteen shows in all. And this has been won in spite of a greater number of both Colourpoints and exhibitors at these shows than in previous years. And the USA provides similar results. Ch. Mingchiu Sebastian is the C.F.A. 'best of breed' and also 'best of colour in the Seal-points' for the North Atlantic Region 1968, while his brother Ch. Mingchiu Murdock (Photographs 21a, b) has been scored the 1968 'Gulf Shore Region Best Himalayan', also by the C.F.A. For the 1968–9 season Murdock, with his more mature mask (Photograph 21b) was Best Seal-point Himalayan and B.O.X. Himalayan for the All Southern Region. Both of these cats have anything but equal quantities of Siamese and Persian genes, if they had they would not meet with such approval by the judges! Further, Gr. Ch. Mingchiu Pearlas of Harobed has maintained her position as a top-scoring Himalayan for the Eastern Region of the USA for several successive seasons, besides gaining All-American awards.

The deep-blue eye seen in Siamese, Birmans and some Colourpoints is controlled by genes which are incompletely linked with those determining the long straight nose. It is easy to get this deep-blue colour in Colourpoints when the nose is too long and straight for a good type Longhair (Colour photograph X). Very many of the early Colourpoints had such eyes. Many of the long-nosed American Himalayans also possess the good eye colour, and for the same reason. But with progressive breeding for improvement in type of Colourpoints the eye in most cases loses the good blue (Colour photograph II). This shows up even in the genetical segregation taking place in the formation of one litter, the best typed kitten with a short, well-demarcated nose, usually has poorer eye colour than the siblings who may not be so 'good looking'.

The apparent colour of the eye of a cat, or of any other mammal, ordinarily depends upon the iris. In bright light the pupil in the middle of the iris is small and the iris itself is expanded so that its coloration is visible. In dim light extreme dilatation of the pupil renders the iris almost invisible. Pigment is situated in the iris, and, invisibly from the outside, in other parts of the eyeball as well (retina and choroid). Pigment lying in the outer epithelium of the iris may be the only colouring matter present, but nearly always there are pigment cells also in the substance (stroma) of the iris, which contain various amounts of melanin (a dark brown pigment), coloured oils, or guanin and related substances, which give metallic appearances of silver,

39

gold or colours due to interference or partial absorption of light. As often as not the colour of an iris depends both on pigments and on interference phenomena.

A vivid eye colour may be due to absorption of certain wavelengths of light in the superficial layers of the iris, together with differential reflection of only some of the remaining wavelengths, the rest being absorbed in the deeper tissues of the iris. The green spots on a frog's skin and the blue eye of a cat are produced in this way, not by either green or blue pigments.

In blue eyes the brown pigment lying over the internal (hinder) face of the iris is the only pigment present in the iris. The apparent blueness is caused by optical effects similar to those which make veins, containing dark red blood, appear blue when seen through white skin. Brown and black eyes result from pigment being situated in the substance of the iris. In an albino the pigment is lacking in both the iris and the retina, so that the pink blood vessels become visible through the tissues, resulting in an iris which appears to be pink[1].

It is much more difficult to establish good type than good eye colour. The inheritance of eye colour is not simple, and does not appear to be determined by the same genes in all varieties of cats possessing blue eyes. The blue in Colourpoints is recessive, as in man, thus good blue must be carried visibly or invisibly (homozygous or heterozygous) by both parents if there is to be any chance of good blue occurring in the offspring. But it is useless to try to make progress in Colourpoint breeding by selecting from the progeny of two blue-eyed, long-nosed Colourpoints. The result is seen in large numbers of American Himalayans as well as in our own experimental breeding. Good type must be established first and the eye colour can be attended to later.

The colour of the eyes of Colourpoints descended directly from Self-coloured Longhair carriers is often, but not always, poor. Both Ch. Mingchiu Tinka and Ch. Mingchiu Obel (Colour photographs II, IV) have black Longhair mothers and pale eye colour. The blue, however, can be restored by subsequent Colourpoint to Colourpoint

---

[1]A fine account of eyes can be found in Walls, G. L., 1942, *The Vertebrate Eye and its Adaptive Radiation*, Cranbrook Inst. Sci. U.S.A. 19. i–xiv, 1–785, 197 textfigs.

8

9

GROWTH OF TYPE AND EARS
Compare with Photographs 4–7 opposite p. 25.

Above: Gr. Ch. Mingchiu Nootka of Pic's, a Blue-pointed female at 2 months showing the small ears and inextensive mask typical of young kittens, the fine type and coat. *Below:* A fine Blue-pointed kitten bred by Mrs M. Wright, aged 4 months, an age when the adult quality is first clearly detectable.

10   TYPE IN MALES
Ch. Mingchiu Choc at 2 years, with fine coat, intensely blue eyes, ears a little too large, but well set.

Ch. Mingchiu Ghunti in his first winter coat which is longer than that of some subsequent winters (cf. Colour photograph VII), note his very wide short nose and small, well-set ears.

12

NINE YEARS OF PROGRESS
An early breeding Colourpoint in the Mingchiu cattery at 8 months, 1958.
Compare with Photograph 13 opposite p. 72.

matings. E.g. Ch. Mingchiu Chou-lu (Photograph 3), the winning Colourpoint at the National Show 1967 has very good blue eyes, in spite of his black grandmother, who gave him his fine type. His eye colour exceeds that of his mother and father. Eye colour in Ch. Mingchiu Mudoba is finer still (Colour photograph I). The cause of the loss of the blue eye colour on outcrossing to a Self-coloured Persian or Longhair is simply the acquisition of pigment in the substance and front surface of the iris, but not to the full extent as to give an orange colour to the eye. It is undesirable to make a series of successive outcrosses to Self-coloured Longhairs because so much of the visual blue eye colour is lost thereby.

A fine blue can best be produced by mating cats together which each carry good eye colour (Colour photographs I, III, V, IX). Kittens from a pair of Colourpoints, each with deep-blue eyes, will not all be the same in this respect, a range of intensity turning up, with only an occasional outstanding deep-blue-eyed cat. But deep blue can arise from less blue-eyed parents, e.g. Ch. Mingchiu Choc (Photograph 10), with intense blue eyes, arose from Mingchiu Snuff (Chocolate-point) and Briarry Tromo (Seal-point), neither of whom had more than pale blue eyes. It is not true that intensity of blue eye colour is linked with intensity of points colour, as sometimes stated. Intensely blue eyes can be obtained with Chocolate (Colour photograph IX) and Lilac-points, although the eye colour of these varieties is often pale (Colour photograph XII).

Good blue eyes in Colourpoints can also be obtained by outcrossing to Siamese, but after that step (Photograph 31), many generations of breeding are needed to eliminate the Siamese characteristics, thereby brought in, and to restore the Longhair type. But it can be done by this method. The linkage between the long straight nose and eye colour has been dissociated in the Mingchiu cattery and the deep-blue eye colour of the Siamese has been introduced into the short nosed type. The original purpose of a Siamese outcross concerned the introduction of the genes for chocolate (brown), as described in Chapters 6 and 7, and the improvement in eye colour came along with this breeding programme. We now have Ch. Mingchiu Merle and Ch. Mingchiu Mudoba (Colour photograph I) with eyes as intensely blue as any Siamese, combined with a short, well-demarcated nose and good top to the head which have delighted all

41

their judges. The Mingchiu Chocolate and Lilac-points now either have reasonably good eye colour, or they carry it. Mingchiu Tiree, Seal-point, has the same blue eyes as Merle and with others has played a large part in the development of the Chocolate and Lilac-points in England. It must be emphasized that progressive breeding of this nature takes much time, energy and money, because several parallel matings and lines of breeding must be maintained, but it has produced results.

Ch. Mingchiu Chou-Lu, with his cobby body, wide head with short, well-demarcated nose, very small outwardly directed ears (except when he pricks them), firm chin, short tail and legs, pale body colour, dark points, fine blue eyes, soft silky coat five inches in length on the back, flanks and frill and longer on the short brush, has pressed our finest specimens of other Longhair varieties very hard for the highest honour of best Longhair cat in show, and he is not the only one to do this. An outstanding grandson of the blue-eyed Mingchiu Tiree has improved upon Chou-Lu. Mingchiu Mudoba has won his adult open class and a championship certificate every time shown, seven occasions during the 1968–9 season. He has pressed the nominees for best Longhair cat in show in progressive measure with increase in age, and became runner up and finally the winner of this highest and most coveted award in March 1969 at the age of only 13½ months.

Colourpoint kittens have on several occasions also achieved the highest placing. Out of the first ten shows of the 1967–8 season a Colourpoint kitten has been best Longhair kitten in show on five occasions, three different kittens making these wins. As there are at least 14 different varieties of Longhairs it seems that Colourpoints have either won more than their share or that their quality has been outstanding.

The above achievements of cats and kittens indicate the progress that has been made in a short span on the lines of breeding here described. The present and future development of the different colours of the points is considered in Chapters 6–8.

Colourpoints, however fine they may be genetically, may not be magnificent in appearance all the year round, or even at all, because a fine coat growth is seasonal at best, and may not occur when the cat lives indoors under unsuitable conditions of heat and dryness and lack of exercise, etc. Generally the coat is shed once a year, usually in the spring, and a new coat is grown by the following winter. A moult once started is not hindered by weather, and cold following the onset of a moult usually will not stop it. Some cats moult early in the winter, regularly in December for Ch. Mingchiu Monique, and others do not start until February or March. The adolescents mostly moult at the age of about a year, regardless of the seasons. Some Colourpoints moult slowly, hair by hair, over a long period and at all times have quite impressive coats. Others moult heavily at one time, and go through a period of being short, almost as short as a Shorthair, on head and shoulders. Many of the Mingchiu cats are in this state in September and it takes them until December or later to reach a full coat. Some fine cats during their first adult summer appear to shed much of their good type as well as coat, a most disconcerting phenomenon for the owner. But they regain their good looks later on. Thus, at the beginning of the show season in August to November, the mature cats are not enough in coat to 'show', and the prizes go to the adolescents just over 9 months of age, so qualifying as adults, before their first moult sets in. A moult in which a considerable area of hair falls out completely, or is scratched off by the cat, spells ruination to the next coat, because the denuded skin becomes cold and the new growth is very dark in colour, giving local, most undesirable, dark patches. These are not permanent and the pale colour can be restored at the next moult. Often the hair becomes bleached before falling out, or individual hairs may become banded, giving an undesirable brindling to the mask and tail. Brindling can also be caused by ill health.

In the case of females, one cannot have both coat and kittens. If a Colourpoint breeds young and keeps it up, the nature of her potential coat may never show until she gives herself a break in the autumn or late summer from the production of kittens, this being a time of year when the coat will grow if unhampered by maternity. Briarry Jehane is such a cat, and in her sixth year she grew a frill and a long silky coat for the first time, a coat that would have gained her a championship in her youth had she grown it then.

The names of many of the Briarry cats aptly express either their characters or indicate progress or otherwise towards improvement in type. There were Swashbuckler and Bizbod, whose names appear in the background on many pedigrees. The disappointing girl Uglia, with the accent on the i, was the daughter of Ugly. By contrast the queen Far Neerah was a decided step in the right direction. There is great scope for ingenuity in the naming of cats!

The initial mixing of the genes for Longhair and Siamese has, by means of selection and outcrossing to Longhairs, given rise to the best-typed Colourpoint, which by 1969 is almost entirely Longhair in its genetical make up for type. It is equally possible to select in the opposite direction and to outcross to Siamese and thereby to produce a Longhair cat possessing say 99·9 per cent of genes for Siamese type and colour pattern and 0·1 per cent for Longhair coat. The American Balinese cat appears to be roughly such a cat, but none have been bred in England by 1969. A middle course can also be adopted, and with the addition of the genes for white feet (see p. 81), the result is a Birman. However, it must not be supposed that it is equally simple to produce a cat with any desired combination of characters. When genes are located on the same bearer, or chromosome, the phenomena of linkage, partial linkage, sex linkage, etc. occur, so that the type of segregation of genes, which takes place before each new generation of cats is produced, differs from that described above.

What may be expected of Colourpoint breeding of the future? In the Mingchiu cattery and in others it will go along the same lines as described above. Further improvement in type is to be expected, so that in a few years the average well-bred Colourpoint will be like our very best today.

It has been stated outside England that Colourpoints (Himalayans) cannot be propagated indefinitely without outcrossing to Siamese, because the body becomes dark and indistinguishable from the points. Colourpoints have been bred in Richmond, Surrey for more years than in any other part of the world. The Mingchiu cats all have singularly pale body colour, such as is sought after the world over, and their ancestry shows not one outcross to Siamese except in respect of the Chocolate and Lilac-points. There are various ways of getting the undesirable dark body colour, indoor dry heat of a high level is one of them, and drinking water affecting the thyroid gland may be another. All Seal and Blue-pointed Colourpoints darken slightly on the body in the second winter, and to different degrees in different individuals. Rarely the coat remains entirely pale, as in Ch.

Mingchiu Monique, who at 8 years of age was as pale as at 8 months (Photograph 22). When the points are deeply pigmented slight darkening on the body after the age of 2 years is in order, but when the points are lightly pigmented a darkening of the body leaves insufficient contrast between points and trunk (Colour photograph VII). Some of the winter darkening is dispelled in the following summer, but usually a little remains.

Occasionally kittens are born with much darker coats than the average. These occur sporadically, or rarely whole litters may be dark in body colour. In examples that have passed through the Mingchiu and Briarry catteries the darkening has passed away entirely, and by late kittenhood the coat has become pale as in the average kitten or adult. It should be noted that other varieties of cat show curious and temporary kitten coats. Longhair Black kittens are occasionally black, but usually they are brownish or grey, at least in part. As a kitten Mingchiu Meg, a Colourpoint carrier, had a black face, legs and tail and the body coat was grey tipped with silver. She was most striking, like a black kitten hidden in a silver muff, but it all passed away when she moulted to a good adult black all over.

An outcrossing to Siamese is the last thing to be recommended in breeding Colourpoints because so much type is lost thereby, and a large number of subsequent generations of selective breeding is required to eliminate the unwanted Siamese characters brought in by such a mating. Factors for the blue eye may be introduced this way, but at a great loss of type.

The standard of points recognized for Colourpoints in Britain by the Governing Council of the Cat Fancy follows the original aim of the breeders to produce a Longhair (or Persian) cat with the Siamese colour pattern.

The Standard for the Colourpoint Longhair Cat

Coat: Fur long, thick and soft in texture; frill full. Colour to be Seal, Blue, Chocolate or Lilac-pointed, with appropriate body colour as for Siamese (i.e. cream, glacial white, ivory or magnolia). Points to be of solid colour, and body shading, if any, to tone with the points. (Colour photographs I, III, Photographs 2, 3, 13, 17, 18, 23). (The Red and Tortie-pointed Colourpoints have not been recognized yet).

45

Head: Broad and round with width between ears. Short face and short nose, with a distinct break or stop. Ears small and tufted and cheeks well developed (Photographs 1, 9, 18, 21, 23).

Eyes: Shape: large, round and full. Colour: clear, bright and decidedly blue (Colour photographs I–VII, Photographs 1, 34).

Body: Cobby and low on leg (Colour photographs V, VIII and XI).

Tail: Short and full, not tapering. A kink shall be considered a defect (Colour photographs II, V, VIII and XI).

N.B. Any similarity in *type* to Siamese, particularly a long straight nose, to be considered most undesirable and incorrect.

Scale of Points

Coat	15
Points and body colour	10
Head	30
Shape of eye	10
Colour of eye	10
Body	15
Tail	10
	100

It is seen that the number of marks given to eye colour is far less than those given for type. It is very easy to breed a Colourpoint of poor type with a long nose, but a bright blue eye, and much less easy to produce a good blue eye with the best type. The only satisfactory procedure is to work for good type first and the eye colour can be attended to later. The attractiveness of the good blue eye combined with the finest coat and Persian type is great, and worth all the work in breeding that will achieve it.

No mention is made in the G.C.C.F. Standard of the colours of the pads on the feet. This feature is out of place in any standard because the colours change during the life of the cat, there is much variation, and the colour of the points cannot be ascertained by inspection of the pads. There is also no mention of any dark mark on the belly. A standard should emphasize the important features of conformation and colour, and it should never provide loopholes for judgment of cats upon features such as pad colour and other unimportant features instead of the much more difficult items of type. The simple standard of the G.C.C.F. has been accepted by all European countries. If universal standards are called for, no approval from Europe can be expected for the elaborate and in part erroneous standards to be found in America.

5. Hybrids, mutations and the status of the Colourpoint Longhair Cat

Strictly speaking, it is quite wrong to apply the term 'hybrid' to a cross between two varieties of the same species, such as a Siamese and a Longhair cat. The term hybrid is not misused in respect of many other domestic animals, so why should it be misused by cat fancies? A hybrid is the F 1 (first filial generation) resulting from the mating between two different species, and is usually sterile, e.g. a mule resulting from the mating of a horse and a donkey. Still more wrong is the application of the term hybrid to a Colourpoint. The F 3, F 4, F 5, F 6, etc. generations from an original cross between two varieties of one species, and selected heavily at each generation in favour of one of the original varieties, leads to the almost total exclusion of the other. A good type Colourpoint is as Persian or Longhair as any other colour variety of such cats, but has the gene for a coat pattern existing elsewhere only in the Birman and Siamese. The latter is called a 'Foreign' type in England as opposed to the 'British Shorthair' which possesses a short coat, but otherwise opposite characters. The Siamese colour pattern could be introduced into the 'British' type with its round face, stocky body, etc. just as it has been introduced into the Longhair. The genetical make up of the ideal Colourpoint, towards which we are now closely approaching, is one with nothing but Persian or Longhair genes besides those controlling the appearance of the colour pattern. No cat fancy wants to call a Blue Persian a 'hybrid' because the colour blue occurs also in both 'British' and 'Foreign' Shorthairs. Yet such a move would be no more ridiculous than the practice of calling a Himalayan a 'hybrid'. It is all but unbelievable that at the present day responsible bodies, which lay down the laws of the cat fancies, should be so ignorant of the well established facts of animal breeding as to make such blunders, and thereby to hamstring the breeding of Colourpoints or Himalayans in their countries.

The worship, in certain quarters, of many similar successive

IV THE CREAM OF BRITISH COLOURPOINTS IN 1969
Above: Ch. Mingchiu Obel, female Seal-point whose type is unsurpassed, is at 12 months in summer. Her mask is not fully developed and her coat is less well groomed than in Colour photograph III.
V *Below*: Ch. Mingchiu Mudoba showing his cobby body, short legs, short tail and large frill (see also Colour photograph I).

generations of cats is another real hindrance to progressive breeding of Colourpoints or of Himalayans. The idea stems from not understanding that a cat with visible recessive characters is pure for those characters, and no further generations can make it any purer. Further generations of the same simply result in time wasted in maintaining the existing facies of Himalayan or Colourpoint, as within a pure line (see above p. 31), without much progress towards the full Persian or Longhair type.

Further, it is not sufficiently appreciated that absolute purity of breeding stock cannot be obtained, however many generations may be recorded in the files of Registrars. We have dealt above with Longhair cats which carry the gene for Siamese colour pattern, but are otherwise indistinguishable from other Longhair cats of the same variety which do not. It is only by outcrossing these carriers to suitable mates that the existence of the recessive genes is disclosed. In the breeding of pedigree stocks of our domestic varieties it is not customary to make outcrosses between widely different varieties, such as Longhair and Shorthair. And unless such crosses are made, no indication is given as to the presence or absence of recessive genes. Owners and registrars just do not know if they are present or not. In other words, hundreds of generations can pass and the animals may be believed to be 'pure bred'. Nobody dreams of calling, say, a pedigree Black champion a 'hybrid' because he may or may not carry some unknown recessive genes not shown on the pedigree. All our pedigree stocks might be labelled 'hybrids' if the possible presence of recessive genes was considered.

To give but one concrete example: Many generations of distinguished Siamese cats have been recorded by a cat fancy forming the pedigree of a well-known champion. For reasons unconnected with perpetuating first rate Siamese cats, this stud was outcrossed to a Longhair. Naturally only Shorthair kittens were expected, the stud being believed to be 'pure'. Actually one Longhair kitten was born, showing that this 'pure' line of Siamese cats was actually carrying the recessive gene for Longhair in at least some of its members. Had the outcross never been made, we should have had no knowledge of the existence of the recessive gene in the Siamese cat and the stock would have been considered to be 'pure'.

It is impossible to make any meaningful classification or qualification of cats showing dominant characters which takes note of the innumerable recessives which they may or may not be carrying. Recessive genes which are carried through very many generations in the heterozygous, or single, state do not become less potent in calling forth the visible features when these genes have the opportunity to become homozygous (present in double dose). The idea that genes fade in potency, when carried through generation numbers of the order used and known in our breeding programmes, is unfounded upon scientific facts, although stated to be so by certain breeders who have little appreciation of genetics and cannot substantiate the claim.

Some cat fancies register a Black Longhair cat as such, just as they register a Siamese, regardless of the possible presence in both of recessive characters, such as a gene for the Siamese pattern in the Longhair and a gene for Longhair in the Siamese. It is not logical to draw a line between the presence of a known recessive character, disclosed perhaps by some quite unorthodox mating, and the probable presence of an unlimited and vast array of unknown ones in the cats for registration. It is quite absurd to call, for example, a Black, Blue or Brown Longhair carrying the Colourpoint or Siamese coat pattern a 'hybrid' or a 'Himalayan'. Such cats are decidedly not Himalayan, nor are they hybrids, they are genetically unlike the latter and carry only one gene for the patterned coat and not two. (They are heterozygous). Yet we have cat fancies who confuse the issue to such an extent as to classify Longhair Black, Blue and Brown cats with solid colours (Self-coloured) as 'Himalayan'. No greater contradiction in terms could be devised, nor a greater disservice rendered to the breeders.

It follows that absolute purity in all characters is almost a fiction, certainly as far as much of our legislation goes, e.g. on the importation of 'pure-bred' animals into a country, or the 'purity' of any one variety to a cat fancy. Attempts have been made over the years to breed mice as homozygous as possible for all genes, that is to produce absolutely pure strains. Such mice are useful for many purposes because they are all alike. But the result is an animal with very low fecundity and, as generations go by, they become very difficult to breed at all.

In the cat fancies the unqualified word 'purity', applied to large categories or varieties, should be expurgated as meaningless, and in place the concept 'pure for, what' should be considered. And, as we certainly do not want our domestic varieties to become sterile and almost impossible to breed, we do not want them pure for as many genes as possible as some cat fancies would like, that would spell disaster. It is time that cat fancies in general became more familiar with the facts of animal breeding. It is no use producing legislation contrary to these facts because the animals will not obey. And the cats will charm us most when unfettered by ill conceived legislation. Legislation, of course, we must have, but let it be based upon up-to-date knowledge.

It has been shown above how segregation and reassortment of genes gives rise to varieties of cat which are different from their parents. The formation of domestic varieties such as Colourpoint (see above) or Self-chocolate Longhair (see Chapter 7) is due to nothing new, the genes determining these varieties being present, but their effects masked, in other existing varieties. This type of origin of new varieties, by a reshuffle of existing genes, is not at all the same thing as a new variety arising by a 'mutation'. This term has been misused by cat fancies just as much as has the word 'hybrid'.

A real change in the gene complex of an animal, which is not a re-shuffle of existing genes, sometimes occurs. It can be induced by radiations, etc., but naturally occurring it is very rare. A mutation of a gene, as these changes are called, are inherited in the manner already described for any genetical character. Mutations are usually, but not always, recessive, and therefore do not usually call forth visible features unless in double dose (homozygous).

A mutation may alter a visible characteristic directly, or it may alter the growth rates of one part relative to another, and this can bring an embryonic feature into the post-embryonic life span of a cat. The latter is the probable explanation of the lop-eared cat, recently bred in Scotland. The appearance of an unexpected type of kitten does not necessarily mean that a mutation has occurred, as is not infrequently claimed in the cat fancy. An example of the misuse of the term 'mutation' is shown by the following quotation from *Cats* magazine, Feb. 1968, p. 14: 'The Longhair Manx Mutation is considered a mutant because these kittens have been born to parents with seven or more complete generations of registered Manx in their backgrounds . . . . Since short hair is said to be dominant over long, two longhaired Manx bred to each other—were they not mutations—would tend to produce some shorthaired kittens. In the case of the Longhaired Manx mutations this has never happened'. This statement is far from supporting the view that there has been a mutation for Longhair among the Manx cats! No pair of longhaired cats, Manx or any other variety, will 'tend to produce some shorthaired kittens'. Short hair is dominant to long and if you have long hair at all you have it pure, i.e. homozygous for long hair. Seven or any other number of generations of Manx is no proof that some of these cats are not heterozygous for hair length, and until two Manx cats, each heterozygous for the genes producing long hair, are mated together, no longhaired Manx will be produced. There is nothing more remarkable in breeding a longhaired Manx than in breeding a longhaired kitten from the long line of Siamese mated to a Longhair noted above p. 49, or in obtaining a Colourpoint by mating two shorthaired carriers together, e.g. those on Squares 7 and 10 in the table on p. 27.

In Britain the aim of Colourpoint breeding has been, from the beginning, to produce and develop a Longhair or Persian cat with the Siamese colour pattern. Therefore no legislative difficulties have been thrust upon breeders by their cat fancy, since the G.C.C.F. appreciates the genetical similarity between Colourpoints and other varieties of Persian or Longhair. If all Colourpoints are not yet 99·9 per cent Persian in their genetical make up in 1969, it is only a matter of time before they may become so. The Self-chocolate and Self-lilac (Frost) Longhairs (Colour photographs XIII, XIV, XV) will soon claim recognition as two more colour varieties of Longhair or Persian, when they have passed through a few more generations. There will be no occasion to regard the Chocolate (Brown) or Lilac Longhairs as differing in any way, besides colour, from the Blue (Photograph 14), Black and other coloured Longhairs. If no Longhair Blues existed, they could easily be made by introducing the genes for blue dilution from Shorthairs. The genetical composition of such 'synthetic' Blue Longhair would be identical with those which are actually in existence. The making of 'synthetic' Blue Longhair would exactly parallel the breeding programmes which have actually taken place during the formation of Self-lilac, Self-chocolate and Colourpoint Longhairs (see also Chapters 6–8). These three varieties are genetically just as much colour varieties of Persian as are any of the older established colour varieties of Longhair.

No such easy and enlightened legislations faces the breeders of Himalayans in the USA. While the conflicts go on as to whether Himalayans are Persians, hybrids, something independent or special, breeders are hampered by legislation which appears to embody no appreciation of feline genetics. Yet in spite of this the appearance on the show benches of a few imported Colourpoints of good type has brought the names of these cats to the annual lists of top scorers for that continent, for example: Mingchiu Murdock and others for the South, Mingchiu Tal and Mingchiu Pearlas for the East, Mingchiu Nookka for the north-west of Canada, Mingchiu Pearlas, also an All-American winner, Mingchiu Sebastian (see above) and others. Several are Grand Champions, and in 1969 the leading cattery prefix for the sectional winners of the north American continent is Mingchiu, with ten wins. The judges are in no doubt whatever as to what they like best, even if some cat fancies state that Himalayans are not Persians. It has been said (*Cats* magazine, May 1968) that some American breeders of Persian cats do not want the Himalayan included under the heading of Persian. But it should be recognized that the nature of existing Himalayans can never be determined by what some people do or do not want, but only by what they are, genetically and in fact.

It is remarkable that one small garden on the outskirts of London, which has carried on from the start made by the Briarry cattery, has produced results reaping world wide acclamation. The sooner it is appreciated that talk and regulations cannot alter the genetical make up of the Colourpoints claimed by American judges to be the finest Himalayans they have handled, the better it will be for American breeders. Successful competition with Colourpoints will occur when Himalayans become more fully Persian in their genetical make up. Whether they do this or not depends upon the aims of the breeders, how the breeding is carried out and what legislation has to be faced. English Colourpoints have been imported into Canada and the USA, but not primarily to provide new blood, as sometimes stated. There is plenty of new blood on that continent. They are imported because of their show-bench potential. And every time a Colourpoint of good type is mated to a Himalayan, the genetically Persian content of the

53

progeny is increased, no matter what the legislation may be! American breeders and cat fancies cannot honestly claim that they can produce a cat, which their own judges will find superior to top winning Mingchiu Colourpoints, which is not more than 50 per cent Persian in its genetical make up. Such a concept is contrary to the facts. If they wish, breeders of Himalayans could decide not to breed towards the British G.C.C.F. standard of points for Colourpoints which is accepted by all of Europe, and make some other kind of cat which does not resemble a Persian in its conformation. But this step would be in an opposite direction from the selection being exercised at the present time.

6. The inheritance of Seal, Blue, Chocolate and Lilac colours of the points of Colourpoints

Some of the early Colourpoints in the Briarry cattery were descended from a Colourpoint found as a stray, Bubastis Georgina, and presumably produced from chance matings of the type described above. Bubastis was mated to a Black Longhair, Kala Sabu, invisibly carrying both Blue and the Siamese colour pattern, and bred by Miss Collins. This cat was an F 2 descendant from a mating between a Seal-pointed Siamese and an unregistered Blue Longhair. Seal-point may be taken as the basic colour of the Colourpoint coat pattern. The dark brown of the points corresponds with the Black of the Self-coloured cats (Colour photographs V, XI, Photograph 20). A Blue-pointed cat has in addition to the genes controlling the Seal-pointed colouring, genes in duplicate causing a dilution of the seal colour which becomes blue-grey, a colour called Blue in cats (Colour photographs III, VII, Photographs 22, 23). Seal and Blue-pointed cats are seen side by side in Photographs 6, 7, 19. Blue is described as recessive to Seal, because a cat carrying but one of the genes for blue dilution is visibly seal-pointed. Since the cats originally used in Colourpoint breeding include Blue (Photograph 14) and Black (resembling Photograph 20) Longhairs, the resulting Colourpoints were both Seal and Blue-pointed.

The following symbols, which are in general use, provide a working representation of the genetical composition of certain varieties of cat of interest in the present connection.

Black Shorthair (Photograph 15)[1]   *aa*

Black Longhair (Photograph 20)   *aall*, bearing in addition two genes for Longhair, *ll*.

Blue Longhair (Photograph 14)   *aalldd* possesses also a pair of genes *dd* causing dilution of the seal colour to blue.

[1]The symbol *aa* really denotes the absence of agouti ticking of the fur, such as is present in the Tabbies, Abyssinian and Chinchilla cats. The agouti factor is almost absent in the red points of both Siamese and Colourpoint.

Seal-pointed Colourpoint (Colour Photograph II)	$aallc^sc^s$ is genetically like the Longhair Black, but with the addition of a pair of genes c^sc^s evoking the Siamese coat pattern.
Blue-pointed Colourpoint (homozygous for blue)	$aallc^sc^sdd$ bears in addition the pair of genes for Blue dilution, *dd*.
Seal-pointed Colourpoint carrying blue (heterozygous for blue)	$aallc^sc^sd-$, only one gene for Blue dilution being present.

The inheritance and segregation of Seal and of Blue-pointed Colourpoints takes place as shown above, Blue being visual only when homozygous, in double dose. For example, if two Seal-points carrying Blue are mated together:

SEAL-POINTED COLOURPOINT   ×   SEAL-POINTED COLOURPOINT

CARRYING BLUE, FEMALE   CARRYING BLUE, MALE

$aallc^sc^sd-$ $aallc^sc^sd-$

The eggs will be: The sperms will be:

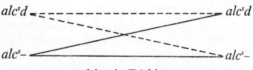

alc^sd alc^sd

alc^s- alc^s-

resulting in F 1 kittens:

$aallc^sc^sdd$ $aallc^sc^sd-$ $aallc^sc^sd-$ $aallc^sc^s--$

one pure Blue-point   two Seal-points carrying   one pure Seal-point

blue invisibly

It may be useful to summarize the results of making various matings between Colourpoints with different coloured points.

Seal-point when pure and mated to any other colour of point will give only Seal-point progeny.

Blue-point mated to *Blue-point* will give only Blue-point progeny.

A Seal-point carrying blue (e.g. Ch. Mingchiu Polo (Photograph 1)) and mated to the *same* (e.g. Briarry Roxana), will give one Blue-point in four, and three Seal-points being one pure and two carriers of Blue (see above). Seven litters actually obtained:

(1) 2 Seal-points, 2 Blue-points   (5) 4 Seal-points

(2) 4 Seal-points   (6) 4 Seal-points

(3) 4 Seal-points, 2 Blue-points   (7) 2 Seal-points, 2 Blue-points

(4) 2 Seal-points, 1 Blue-point

A Seal-point carrying Blue and mated to a Blue-point will give half the progeny Blue-point and half will be Seal-point carrying Blue.

A visual Blue-point is pure for Blue because it will not be visible unless the gene for Blue dilution is homozygous, in double dose. A visual Seal-point can be either pure, or it can carry Blue (and/or Chocolate, see below), and it is possible to differentiate these cats only by further breeding. The majority of our Seal-points do in fact carry Blue but not all do so.

Lilac and Chocolate-pointed Colourpoints possess the Chocolate or Brown gene which occurs also in Chocolate-pointed Siamese and in Self-Chocolate Shorthairs. The genetical composition of these two varieties of Colourpoint is:

Chocolate-pointed Colourpoint (Colour photograph IX) $aallc^sc^sbb$, a cat resembling the Seal-point genetically, but bearing in addition two genes for Chocolate (Brown) bb. The colour of the points resembles that of milk chocolate and is quite distinct from the brown of the Seal-points (Colour photographs IX, XV).

Lilac-pointed Colourpoint (Colour photograph XII) $aallc^sc^sbbdd$, results from the addition of the blue dilution gene in duplicate to the Chocolate-point, the presence of these latter genes turning the chocolate to lilac just as they dilute the seal to blue. The colour is the palest of the series, but is quite unlike a pale Blue-point because the chocolate tone is visible, although diluted (Colour photographs VIII, XII and XIV).

The inheritance and segregation of the colours of the points is not complex, although it is based upon the additive series of genes listed above. Chocolate and Lilac segregate just as do the Blue-points, see above.

Chocolate-point mated to *Chocolate-point* will give only Chocolate-pointed progeny.

A Seal-point carrying Chocolate (e.g. Ch. Mingchiu Merle) when mated to a *Chocolate-point* (e.g. Ch. Mingchiu Ptan Colour photograph IX), will give half the progeny Chocolate-point and half Seal-point carriers, the Chocolate-pointed cats being pure for Chocolate.

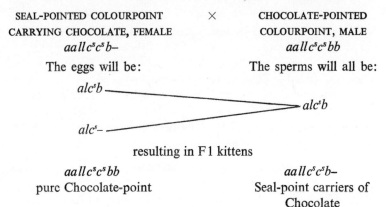

| SEAL-POINTED COLOURPOINT CARRYING CHOCOLATE, FEMALE | × | CHOCOLATE-POINTED COLOURPOINT, MALE |

$aa\,ll\,c^s c^s\,b-$ $\qquad\qquad\qquad$ $aa\,ll\,c^s c^s\,bb$

The eggs will be: $\qquad\qquad$ The sperms will all be:

alc^sb

alc^sb

alc^s-

resulting in F1 kittens

$aa\,ll\,c^s c^s\,bb$ $\qquad\qquad\qquad$ $aa\,ll\,c^s c^s\,b-$
pure Chocolate-point $\qquad\qquad$ Seal-point carriers of
$\qquad\qquad\qquad\qquad\qquad\qquad$ Chocolate

in equal numbers.

A Blue-point carrying Chocolate (e.g. Ch. Mingchiu Chirk (Colour photograph III)) when mated to the *same* (or to a Seal-point carrying Chocolate), will produce one Chocolate-point in four among the progeny, the others being in the proportion of one pure Blue-point (or Seal) and two carriers as above.

A Blue-point carrying Chocolate (e.g. Ch. Mingchiu Chirk) mated to a *Chocolate-point* (e.g. Mingchiu Una) will produce half the progeny with Chocolate points and the other half Seal-point carriers. Two litters actually obtained:

(1) 1 Chocolate-point, 2 Seal-points.
(2) 3 Chocolate-points, 3 Seal-points.

Lilac-point is visual only when the cat is homozygous for both the Chocolate and the Blue dilution genes, both in double dose.

Lilac-point mated to *Lilac-point* produces only Lilac-point (Colour photographs XII, XIV).

Lilac-point (e.g. Mingchiu Sula Three) mated to a *Blue-point carrying Chocolate* (e.g. Ch. Mingchiu Chirk (Colour photograph III) will produce half the progeny Lilac-point and half Blue-point carriers of Chocolate:

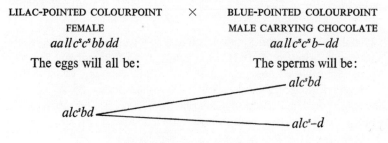

LILAC-POINTED COLOURPOINT FEMALE	×	BLUE-POINTED COLOURPOINT MALE CARRYING CHOCOLATE
$aallc^sc^sbbdd$		$aallc^sc^sb–dd$
The eggs will all be:		The sperms will be:

resulting in F 1 kittens:

$aallc^sc^sbbdd$ — pure Lilac-point

$aallc^sc^sb–dd$ — Blue-point carrying Chocolate invisibly

in equal numbers on the average.

One litter actually obtained: 3 Lilac-points, 2 Blue-point carriers.

Lilac-point mated to a *Seal-point carrying Blue* (e.g. Ch. Mingchiu Shan) will produce no Lilac-points because the Seal is not carrying Chocolate, but if the Seal is carrying Chocolate as well as Blue (Ch. Mingchiu Choc (Photograph 10)), then the progeny will comprise one Lilac-point, one Blue-point carrying Chocolate, one Chocolate-point carrying Blue, and one Seal-point carrying both Blue and Chocolate, on the average.

A male *Blue-point carrying Chocolate* (e.g. Ch. Mingchiu Chirk (Colour photograph III)) mated to a female *Seal-point carrying both Blue and Chocolate* (e.g. Ch. Mingchiu Merle) will produce four types of eggs which will be fertilized by two types of sperms. These combinations, if written out in full, as above, give on the average:

1 kitten in 8: Lilac-point	$aallc^sc^sbbdd$
3 kittens in 8: Blue-point carrying Chocolate	$aallc^sc^sb–dd$
1 kitten in 8: Chocolate-point carrying Blue	$aallc^sc^sbbd–$
1 kitten in 8: Blue-point, pure	$aallc^sc^s--dd$
1 kitten in 8: Seal-point carrying Blue and Chocolate	$aallc^sc^sb–d–$
1 kitten in 8: Seal-point carrying Blue	$aallc^sc^s--d–$

which in external appearance are 1 Lilac-point, 4 Blue-points, 1 Chocolate-point and 2 Seal-points. This proportion of colours was obtained almost exactly in a 1968 litter of seven kittens: 1 Chocolate-point, 1 Lilac-point, 2 Seal-points, 3 Blue-points.

Lilac-point (Mingchiu Sulafour) mated to a *Chocolate-point carrying Blue* (Ch. Mingchiu Ptan (Colour photograph IX)) will give half the progeny Lilac-pointed and half Chocolate carrying Blue. Litter actually obtained: 2 Lilac-points, 3 Chocolate-points.

Lilac-point mated to a Chocolate-point of similar appearance but not carrying Blue will produce only Chocolates carrying Blue.

Colourpoints with Red, Tortie and other coloured points can be produced by suitable matings (see Chapter 8); America is ahead of Britain in their production. The chances against these varieties turning up naturally are rather heavy, but in time they will doubtless appear both with and without human intervention.

The body colour varies according to the colour of the points, as recognized in the Standard, p. 45, and is darkest with the Seal-points. But the coats of all coloured points are usually pale up to the second winter (Colour photographs I, V, VIII, IX, XI, XII). Then the Seal-points usually darken somewhat in the body (Colour photograph X, Photographs 10, 11, 38 left), but not all do so. Any considerable darkening of the body in Blue-points tends to destroy the pleasing contrast between body and points coloration, a condition occurring more frequently in America than in Britain. A Blue-point retaining the completely pale body colour, as in Ch. Mingchiu Monique (Photograph 22), at the age of 7 years, is a very attractive cat. The body colour of the Chocolate and Lilac-points has remained pale (Colour photographs IX, XII, XIV, XV), summer and winter, during the few years in which these varieties have been in existence.

The account of cat genetics presented here has been given in the simplest possible terms for an understanding of the practical matters of Colourpoint breeding. The real picture is somewhat more complex. It has been mentioned that coat length is determined by not one but many superimposed genetical factors. The colour chocolate is incompletely recessive, so that it may 'show through' the Blue-pointed and Seal-pointed coats of the carriers to some extent. The difference in colour between a Blue-point carrying chocolate and one that does not is slight, but it can often just be seen, and similarly for Seal-points which do and do not carry chocolate.

The practice in certain localities of calling a pale or extreme seal-pointed Himalayan a Chocolate-point and a pale Blue-point a Lilac-point is defenceless. There is a range of colour in every category. The extremes of the Seal or Blue-points are not genetically Chocolate or Lilac-pointed at all, and they will not breed these colours. The pedigrees of the cats should show whether there are any real Chocolate or Lilac-points in the last few generations. These colours are very new, and if the pedigree shows none of them, nor any of the short-haired Self or Chocolate-pointed cats from which the Chocolate gene has been obtained, then the genes for chocolate are undoubtedly absent, and to claim that cats are Lilac or Chocolate-pointed is a gross deception. There are cases where cats have been deliberately mal-fed in the hope of changing the colour of the points and creating Lilac or Chocolate. No genetical alterations are made thereby, and the practice is both dishonest and a cruelty to the animals. (See also p. 76).

7. The campaign for the production of Chocolate and Lilac- pointed Colourpoints

The pursuit of Chocolate (Colour photographs IX, XV left) and Lilac-pointed (Colour photographs XII, XIV left) Colourpoints has occupied the full resources of the Briarry and Mingchiu catteries until this goal has been achieved. And a campaign it was. After the necessary initial crosses were made the work progressed with odds of sixteen and thirty-two to one against getting what we wanted. The same matings by the same cats were repeated over and over again, and by different cats with the same genetical makeup, because no cat produces litters of thirty-two kittens, one of which might be the wanted one, or again it might not! A seemingly unending stream of pets was born, each of which had to have a good home found for it. Years went by, but in the end the object was achieved. It took very much longer than the eight years spent in breeding Colourpoints from the beginning in the Briarry cattery up to their recognition by the cat fancy in 1955.

Those who see, acquire or breed a Lilac or Chocolate-point, either ready made, or from ready made stock emanating in the past from the two catteries that have carried on this work, have no idea of the labour and time involved in their background, or of the hopes, disappointments and frustrations that have been endured. The first Chocolate-pointed kitten in the Briarry cattery with good type and full coat met by an untimely end; the first Chocolate-pointed Colourpoint in the Mingchiu Cattery had good type and fine eye colour, but a semi-long coat, much as in a Birman, due to the presence of too many Siamese genes for a good Colourpoint, which had been introduced along with the genes for the colour of the points. And it is no accident that a member of the interested public at one of our largest shows, watching the judging of the first Chocolate-pointed Colourpoint of champion standard, was enchanted by his manners as well as his beauty. So much so, that the home of such cats was sought out. Ch. Mingchiu Ptan, the first Chocolate-pointed Colourpoint Champion (Colour photograph IX), is in the habit of putting his 'arms' round the neck of persons with a friendly smell or manner, judges or anyone else, the better to rub the nose, and he expects his gestures to be reciprocated in some way. Eyes are of far less importance for close-up sensory perception in cats than nose and ears.

Why do we want Chocolate and Lilac-pointed Colourpoints? Is it just the stamp collecting mania for every possible variety of everything? This was not the initial motive. These colours were bred because of their expected beauty in the Longhair, and largely because we expected the body colour to remain pale throughout life, and not darken somewhat, as do most of the Seal and Blue-points. And the pale body colour combined with the dark points, shown during the first eighteen months or so of our old established Colourpoints, is the body colour most sought after by potential owners and breeders, and then, unfortunately, often but not always, found to be evanescent. This forecast of the appearance of cats whose genetical composition was being purposely made has proved to be quite accurate, and these new colour varieties of Colourpoints do maintain a pale body colour throughout life, at least in the several years that any one of them has so far been in existence. A cat past its second winter is not likely to change appreciably in colour. There is a very slight darkening on the back of Chocolate-points in winter, but it pales again in summer and is not sufficient to spoil the general effect. A Lilac-pointed Colourpoint, Mingchiu Sula, at four years of age, was just as pale on the body as in her first season, and Mingchiu Sula Three at $2\frac{1}{2}$ years and Mingchiu Sulafour at eighteen months are like Sula.

The gene for Chocolate (a Brown of a distinctly different tone to that of Seal) had to be introduced into the Longhairs from Shorthairs, because this colour only existed in the Chocolate-pointed Siamese and in Self-chocolate Shorthairs at the time when this work was started. The production of the Chocolate-pointed Colourpoint from the former follows exactly the same lines as described above for the inheritance of two pairs of characters, but as more than two were usually involved, the segregation of the genes concerned was more complex.

The F 1 cats from a mating between a Chocolate-pointed Siamese and a Seal-pointed Colourpoint resemble poor type Siamese with Seal-points, i.e. too short noses and too small ears, etc. for Siamese.

63

Mingchiu Trivia, a Seal-pointed Shorthair, was such a cat (Photograph 31). The mating together of two such carriers produces a great variety of offspring, short-haired, long-haired, Blue-pointed, Seal-pointed, Chocolate-pointed and Lilac-pointed, if blue is carried also by both parents. But in addition coats intermediate in length appeared, the composite genes for coat length here segregating somewhat to give the intermediate lengths. The chances against getting a Chocolate-pointed Longhair from such a mating are great. But the carriers are of great service.

Briarry Tromo was a Seal-pointed Colourpoint of fair type, with a good long coat, and carrying Chocolate. Trivia and Tromo mated together gave a chance of one in thirty-two of producing what we wanted, but Trivia did not want Tromo! He lived a little distance away and there were males who were her friends and to her liking close at hand. She frustrated us many times by her nonco-operation, but in the end she was successfully mated by Tromo on several occasions, producing several most useful litters.

MINGCHIU TRIVIA	$\times$	BRIARRY TROMO
SHORTHAIR SEAL-POINT FEMALE		COLOURPOINT LONGHAIR, SEAL-
(Photograph 31)		POINTED MALE
		(as in Colour Photograph I)
CARRYING LONGHAIR, BLUE		CARRYING CHOCOLATE AND
AND CHOCOLATE		BLUE
$aa\,l-c^s c^s\,b-d-$		$aa\,ll\,c^s c^s\,b-d-$
The eggs will be of eight kinds:		The sperms will be of four kinds:
$alc^s bd$		$alc^s bd$
$alc^s b-$		$alc^s b-$
alc^s-d		alc^s-d
alc^s--		alc^s--
$a-c^s bd$		
$a-c^s b-$		
$a-c^s-d$		
$a-c^s--$		

These eight different kinds of eggs each have an equal chance of being fertilized by any one of the four different types of sperms, so producing thirty-two different genotypes of cats in the progeny. Two of these will be Chocolate-pointed Colourpoints $aallc^s c^s bb$, one

VI AT HOME AND ABROAD
Above: Ch. Mingchiu Mandarin of Sahadi and his 34 British awards, aged 1 year. He is the first Colourpoint to become an international champion between Great Britain and the USA, 1965.

VII *Below*: Ch. Mingchiu Ghunti, a Blue-pointed male with paler points than in Colour photograph III, but magnificent type, aged 4 years. He has lost his very pale adolescent body colour and has sired many champions.

carrying Blue (with one *d* in addition) and the other pure carrying no Blue, and there will be one Lilac-pointed Colourpoint $aa\,ll\,c^sc^s\,bb\,dd$. But there is also the segregation of coat length, not tabulated here. However, in spite of the heavy odds against success in a few years of breeding, a Chocolate-pointed Colourpoint was obtained. She had good type, fine eye colour but coat not as fine as would have been liked. She carried Blue and was one of the ancestors of the Mingchiu Lilac-points.

Matings, such as those just described, had to be made in parallel and many times over in order to provide suitable pairs for further breeding which would not be too closely related. A battalion of Short and Longhaired queens, patterned and plain, in the Briarry cattery, were mated by Tromo, but in spite of the smaller number of animals in the Mingchiu cattery, it was there that Chocolate and Lilac-pointed Colourpoints first grew up. There was no rivalry over this. Both catteries were working together and it did not matter where the first cats of the new varieties actually appeared.

The other source of the Chocolate gene was from Self-coloured Shorthair and, almost from the beginning, this introduced gene was combined with that from Chocolate-point Siamese.

The antecedents of Briarry Bruno, the first Self-Chocolate Longhair, were:

SEAL-POINTED SIAMESE MALE   ×   SELF-BLUE LONGHAIR FEMALE
(Ch. Briarry Macsuch)   (Debutante of Dunesk)

gave

BLACK SHORTHAIR MALE
(Briarry Swashbuckler)
carrying Longhair, Chocolate and Blue

SELF-CHOCOLATE SHORTHAIR   BLUE LONGHAIR MALE
FEMALE
(Laurentide Brown Prestige)   (Ch. Foxborrow Frivolous)

gave

BLUE SHORTHAIR FEMALE
(Gadeford Kelpie)
carrying Longhair and Chocolate

Swashbuckler mated to Kelpie produced Gadeford Bagheera, a

E

Chestnut Brown (Chocolate) Shorthair male carrying Longhair. He was the sire of Briarry Bruno the first Self-chocolate Longhair, a male of fair type, too long a nose, too large ears and fine coat, but also carrying the Siamese colour pattern from his great great grandfather. The gene for the coat pattern had been transmitted invisibly (one gene only, or heterozygous) through the intervening generations.

Bruno, the Self-chocolate Longhair carrying the patterned coat, was mated to Mingchiu Snuff, a Chocolate-pointed Colourpoint carrying blue, and thereby were produced Self-chocolate and Self-lilac Longhair kittens. Other hazards then took over. Faulty vaccines destroyed all but one of these kittens, Mingchiu Lilak (Self-lilac carrying the patterned coat) alone surviving (Colour photograph XIII). Snuff, her mother, got mixed as to which was tail and which was cord just after her birth and bit the wrong thing. The injury ultimately caused the tail tip to shrivel and drop off. Lilak now goes about with a stiff bottle-brush behind, and on occasion she abruptly about turns and waves this stump at me, a sure sign that she wants something.

The final tragedy was the death of Bruno. He left some Longhair Chocolate females in the Briarry cattery, but no male was produced until Mingchiu Lilak (Self-lilac Longhair) was mated to the first Chocolate-pointed Colourpoint male, Mingchiu Romeo, to produce a fine litter of male and female Self-chocolate Longhairs and three Chocolate-pointed Colourpoints, the winning litter of 'any Colour Longhair' at the Kensington Kitten Show in London, July 1967. The type of all these kittens was fairly good, and the male Self-chocolate Longhair, Mingchiu Kohcoh, is an enormous improvement upon his ancestor Briarry Bruno. Good also are the females Mingchiu Danladi, Mingchiu Koffee and Mingchiu Koca from other lines of breeding, the latter out of Mingchiu Lilak (Self-lilac L.H.) by Ch. Mingchiu Ptan (Chocolate-point (Colour photograph IX)), Koca has as good a short, wide, well demarcated nose as any good Longhair and fine orange-coloured eyes (Colour photograph XV right) but the coat needs to be longer. These females with Briarry Madre Decacaid are being mated by Kohcoh and form the great grandparents of Self-chocolate Longhair kittens of the future who will claim recognition and a breed number because they will show three generations of Chocolate to Chocolate matings on their pedigrees.

Having obtained both Chocolate and Lilac-pointed Colourpoints and the two new Self-coloured varieties of cat, breeding goes on now to improve the type and eliminate still further the unwanted characteristics imported from the Shorthairs. To this end Mingchiu Lilak (Self-lilac carrying Colourpoint pattern (Colour photograph XIII)) was mated to a very fine type Seal-pointed colourpoint carrying blue, Ch. Mingchiu Polo (Photograph 1). From the Blue and Seal-pointed carriers so produced, a very fine male Blue-point carrying Chocolate, Ch. Mingchiu Chirk (Colour photograph III), was selected for further breeding. He was second to Ch. Chou-Lu at the National Cat Club Show in London 1967, an indication as to his excellence in type and has since then been placed above him. Chirk is now mating a harem of young Lilac and Chocolate-pointed Colourpoints and champion carriers of Chocolate (e.g. Ch. Mingchiu Merle). The 1968 season has seen the birth of Chocolate and of Lilac-pointed Colourpoints of the same excellence in type as the Seal and Blue-pointed Colourpoints already in existence. This is a fitting tribute to the initial work of the Briarry cattery and to the sound sense and determination of the late Mr B. A. Stirling-Webb in starting this huge project. The mating of existing Chocolate-points to Chocolate-points, would speed the production in numbers of the new variety, but it is better to stem the pace and breed for good type first. Champions of both Chocolate and Lilac-pointed Colourpoints now exist (Colour photographs VIII, XII), and the first breeding pair of Lilac-points passed to other hands in 1968.

From the welter of genes and of the characters which they evoke, four new varieties of cat have been produced: Chocolate-pointed Longhair, Lilac-pointed Longhair, Self-coloured Chocolate Longhair and Lilac Longhair. Each is pure for the characters by which it is named, and each when mated to the same will produce nothing but the same for an unlimited number of generations. The labour, time and resources expended in making these varieties has been great, but the favours of chance are not always so hard to come by.

In Devon a black-and-white pet of unknown ancestry and her daughter found their own mate on more than one occasion. Whether he was the same each time is not known. All we know is that he, or they, must have carried the genes for Longhair, Chocolate and the Siamese colour pattern, but his external appearance might have been almost anything. His or their kittens included a Birman, a Colourpoint, a white-footed Siamese, Blacks, and a Self-chocolate Longhair! A more unlikely achievement would be hard to conceive. Some of these cats were shown at the South Western Counties Show in 1966. They were not of outstandingly good type, but one would hardly expect to find a potential champion of any of our domestic varieties turning up by the chance matings of a 'pet' instead of by selected matings.

The progeny of the black-and-white cat are easily accounted for on the assumption that a strong-minded Chocolate-pointed Siamese had been busy on the loose in the neighbourhood, creating offspring carrying Chocolate. The genes for the other characteristics are freely present in any population of domestic cats. But it was a remarkable piece of 'chance' for someone to get all these varieties when possessing just one pet cat. The Briarry and Mingchiu catteries could well have done with a little more of this sort of chance.

Another piece of chance is worthy of record. It has been shown above how many years and several generations and lines of breeding were needed to put the recessive Chocolate Brown gene into the Longhairs and obtain also good type. And secondly it has been stressed that most of the varieties of domestic cats have arisen in association with a reshuffle of existing genes and not with mutations (see Appendix). But a real mutation of the dominant Black to the recessive Brown gene has been pinpointed. It is probable that this mutation occurred in one spermatogonium, a cell forming sperms, of Ch. Mingchiu Polo, a Seal-point certainly carrying no chocolate. He has been tested several times by mating to Self-lilac and Lilac-points (cats carrying Chocolate) and has never produced a Chocolate or a Lilac of any kind. But two of Polo's Seal-pointed sons have sired both Chocolate and Lilac-points and Selfs, when mated to a visual Chocolate and a Chocolate carrier. This would be impossible if the two sons did not carry Chocolate. A similar origin of a brown mutation has been recorded in the mouse (Searle, A. G., personal communication) and the above is the probable explanation of the mutation in Polo. As far as is recorded, there is no precise information as to the origin of the Chocolate Brown in Siamese or any other Shorthair. Once it is there, the Brown is inherited on the lines described above.

8. Red, Tortie and Cream-pointed Colourpoints and sex-linked inheritance

It is possible to breed Colourpoints as well as Siamese with colour to the points other than Seal, Blue, Chocolate and Lilac. It has been shown in Chapters 3, 6 and 7 how only two modifying pairs of genetical factors alter the basic Seal-pointed cats to any of the three other colours, according to the representation of these genes. Two series of varieties ensue, (1) the Seal and Blue and, (2) the Seal, Chocolate and Lilac-pointed cats. Red and Tortie-pointed cats do not belong to either of these series. They can be made with greater ease than the Chocolate and Lilac-points because no short-haired cats are needed for their production, and so there need be no loss of type in the making of these colour varieties. Both the Red and the Tortie-point are in existence in America in the Longhairs, and a start is being made for their breeding in Britain. The Red-points differ from good Seal, Blue, Chocolate and Lilac-points in that tabby markings are usually apparent to some extent in the points. These stripes are very difficult to eliminate. The Tortie points show the same colours in the points made up by red, black and cream hairs as in cats bearing the full tortoiseshell colouring all over, and 'a blaze of red or cream running down between the eyes is desirable.'

Both Tortie and Red-pointed Colourpoints are dependent upon a gene which produces yellow by modifying the development of melanism, the black pigment in the hair. The shades of yellow range from pastel yellow to rich red, the latter being well seen in the show type Red Selfs and Red Tabbies. The gene producing yellow is inherited slightly differently from those already considered, because it is borne by one of the sex chromosomes. The cat possesses 19 pairs of chromosomes, one of these being the sex pair of chromosomes, usually designated X and Y, because they are not exactly alike, as are the members of the other 18 pairs of chromosomes. Genes are borne by the X chromosome but not by the Y chromosome. The female cat has two X chromosomes, designated XX, while the male cat has XY

69

chromosomes. At the mating of a male and a female:

MALE   ×   FEMALE

XY   XX

two types of sperm and one type of egg will be produced:

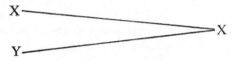

The fertilized eggs will be of two kinds, XX giving female kittens and YX giving male kittens, in equal numbers.

A male with a particular gene in his X chromosome can transmit it to his daughters but not to his sons, while a female with a particular gene in her X chromosomes can transmit it equally to both sons and daughters. Such a gene is described as sex-linked, and the gene O standing for yellow (orange-red) is an example. A female Red Tabby or Red Self (their basic genetical make up is similar) has the gene for yellow in both X chromosomes, designated here $X^O X^O$. The male Red Tabby or Red Self carries but one yellow gene, and his sex chromosomes can be represented $X^O Y$, where the Y chromosome carries no yellow gene. The yellow gene is unlike those so far considered in that it is incompletely dominant and when present on only one X chromosome of the female, XX°, the cat is Tortoiseshell in appearance. The coat is a mixture of yellow and non-yellow hairs, the latter being Tabby or Black. The hair types may be intermingled (brindled) or they may be segregated into areas. There is no Tortoiseshell male because he has only one X chromosome and so the heterozygous state of a Tortoiseshell female never obtains. The Brown Tabby shows no incomplete dominance and the heterozygous state is Tabby not Tortoiseshell in appearance. A mating between Colourpoint and a Brown Tabby produces Tabby and Black kittens in contrast to the results given below from mating a Red Tabby with a Colourpoint.

Two or three generations are needed for the breeding of Colourpoints with Red and Tortie points, but more than one mating of the same kind may be required for obtaining these colours. The start can be made with either a Red Longhair male and a Seal-pointed

Colourpoint female, or the Colourpoint may be the male. The kittens will not be the same in the two crosses, see below. Since both varieties are longhaired, the gene symbols *ll* used above can be omitted because they are present in the homozygous state in all cats and kittens noted below. The symbols $c^s c^s$ as before represent the genes giving the visible Colourpoint coat pattern; when these genes are heterozygous, c^s–, they give a cat carrying the colour pattern invisibly.

RED LONGHAIR MALE   ×   SEAL-POINTED COLOURPOINT FEMALE

$X^O Y$—— $XX c^s c^s$

The sperms will be of two kinds: The eggs will all be:

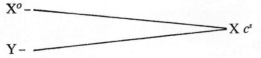

The resulting fertilized eggs and F 1 kittens will be:

$X^O X c^s$– $XY c^s$–

female Tortoiseshells   male Blacks

carrying Colourpoint   carrying Colourpoint

If the cross is made the other way round, using a Red female[1] ($X^O X^O$——) and a Colourpoint male ($XY c^s c^s$), Tortoiseshell female carriers and Red male carriers will be produced.

Now mate one of the Tortoiseshell carriers from either F 1 to a male Colourpoint:

SEAL-POINTED COLOURPOINT   ×   TORTOISESHELL FEMALE

MALE   CARRYING COLOURPOINT

$XY c^s c^s$ $X^O X c^s$–

The sperms will be   The eggs will be

of two kinds: of four kinds:

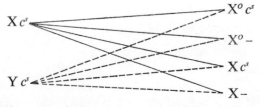

[1]If the Red Selfs were genetically agouti, as are the Tabbies of all colours, Tabbies and Tabby-tortoiseshells would be produced. It is necessary to use Red Selfs that are not carrying agouti.

Each type of egg has an equal chance of being fertilized by either type of sperm, so that four types of females and four types of males will be produced in the F2 generation:

FEMALES

$XX^O c^s c^s$	$XX^O c^s-$	$XX c^s c^s$	$XX c^s-$
Tortie-pointed	Tortoiseshell	Seal-pointed	Black
Colourpoint	carrying	Colourpoint	carrying
female	Colourpoint		Colourpoint

MALES

$X^O Y c^s c^s$	$X^O Y c^s-$	$XY c^s c^s$	$XY c^s-$
Red-pointed	Red carrying	Seal-pointed	Black
Colourpoint	Colourpoint	Colourpoint	carrying
male			Colourpoint

Next, mate together the Red-pointed male Colourpoint produced above in the F2 generation, with a Tortie pointed female Colourpoint from the F2, preferably from a parallel set of matings:

RED-POINTED MALE   ×   TORTIE-POINTED FEMALE
COLOURPOINT   COLOURPOINT
$X^O Y c^s c^s$ $XX^O c^s c^s$

The sperms will be   The eggs will be
of two kinds: of two kinds:

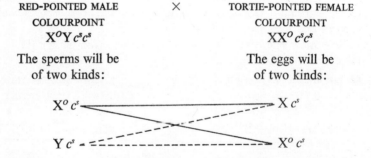

Each egg has an equal chance of being fertilized by either type of sperm, so producing fertilized eggs and F3 kittens:

$XX^O c^s c^s$	$X^O X^O c^s c^s$	$XY c^s c^s$	$X^O Y c^s c^s$
Tortie-pointed	**Red-pointed**	Seal-pointed	**Red-pointed**
female	**female**	male	**male**
Colourpoint	**Colourpoint**	Colourpoint	**Colourpoint**

Thus from one initial outcross of a Colourpoint to a Red Longhair

13

NINE YEARS OF PROGRESS
Ch. Mingchiu Chou-Lu at 8 months, twice best Longhair kitten in show (Harrogate and Southport) later best Colourpoint in Show at the National, 1967. He was sired by Ch. Mingchiu Shan out of Briarry Jehane. His coat reached $5\frac{1}{2}$ inches length. Compare with Photograph 12 opposite p. 41.

14

CONTRIBUTORS TO
COLOURPOINT PROGRESS
Left: Blue Longhair, Ch.
Diana of Pensford. From such
cats bred to Colourpoints invaluable Self-coloured carriers
of the Colourpoint pattern
are produced: these breed both
Self-coloured and Colour-
point kittens.

Right, above: Mingchiu Me-
lania, a Shorthair Black,
carrying the genes for Colourpoint pattern, Blue and
Chocolate. *Below:* Two Mingchiu Black Longhair kittens
of good type, carrying the
Colourpoint pattern, aged 7
weeks.

15

16

17

18

IN PURSUIT OF TYPE
Above and *below:* A budding champion at 11 months, Mingchiu Chou-Lu, showing round wide head and short nose (cf. Photographs 32-33), small, well-set ears and wide top of head, compact body low on the ground, coat $5\frac{1}{2}$ inches and very pale, contrasting with the Seal-points, short, well-furnished brush.

two subsequent generations can produce Red-point males and females and Tortie-point females in the proportions given. However, if two initial outcrosses are made with two Colourpoints, so that a Tortoiseshell carrier and a Red male carrier of Colourpoint are available which are unrelated to one another, then cats with Tortie, and with Red points in both sexes, can all be made in the F2 generation, but at a less advantageous expectation in numbers. A mating between a Tortoiseshell carrier, $X^O X c^s-$, and a Red male carrier, $X^O Y c^s-$, from the F1 litters gives four types of egg and four types of sperm, and the fertilized eggs and resulting kittens will be of 16 types, like the table on p. 27. On average one in 16 will be a Red-pointed female Colourpoint, $X^O X^O c^s c^s$, another will be a Red-pointed male Colourpoint, $X^O Y c^s c^s$, and a third will be a Tortie-pointed female Colourpoint, $X^O X c^s c^s$. The expectation of one of these three types of cat turning up is much less than the one in eight expectation in the F2 or the one in four in the F3 generation from the breeding programme given above in full.

A Red-pointed Colourpoint mated to the same should produce nothing but Red points. A Red-pointed female Colourpoint mated to a Seal-point male will produce Tortie-pointed daughters and Seal-pointed sons.

Tortie-pointed males as well as male Tortoiseshell carriers are unexpected, but they may turn up very rarely, as in the normal Tortoiseshells. Such males as have occurred are usually, but not always, sterile. The genetical explanation of these rare occurrences is open to various alternatives which will not be considered here.

A Cream Longhair is genetically a Red with the addition of homozygous genes for blue dilution dd. Creams can replace Reds in the above breeding programmes, and the F1 cats will carry, but not visibly show, the dilution factor in its heterozygous state $d-$. But if a Cream and a Blue-pointed Colourpoint are used, then Blue-cream carriers of Colourpoint will be formed in the F1, Blue-cream being the dilute form of Tortoiseshell with homozygous genes dd. The continued use of Blue-pointed Colourpoints will lead to the formation of Cream-pointed Colourpoints. Since the availability of Cream Longhairs of good type is greater than that of Reds, the use of good Creams with Seal-pointed Colourpoints should produce satisfactory Red and Tortie-pointed Longhairs. It is further possible

73

that the red colour of the points might be intensified by the use of Chocolate-pointed Colourpoints instead of Seal.

Tabby-pointed Colourpoints could be produced by the incorporation of the genes for blotched, lined or mackerel Tabby into the genetical make up of Colourpoints.

9. The temperament or character of Colourpoints

No account of the heritable characteristics of Colourpoints would be complete without reference to their temperament, on which passing comment has been made in the previous pages. The personality of a cat depends in part upon the genetical make up of the variety. But an enormous amount of individual variation is dependent upon the way the animal is brought up and the manner in which it lives, superimposed of course on the normal character differences between one individual and another, such as are found in any population, or single family, of the animals with considerable intelligence, cat or man.

The general behaviour patterns of Colourpoints are intermediate between those of Siamese and of Self-coloured Persians or Longhairs. There has been plenty of selection of segregating characters affecting the visible structure or colour of cats, but nothing has been purposely done in selection for personality. Colourpoints are on the whole much more enterprising than the average self-coloured cat, and they are a rest cure to an owner who has endured the domineering ways and boisterous and violent affections of the Siamese.

Colourpoints are extremely affectionate, but not as demonstrative or commanding as Siamese. All the same they need and ask much from their owners and do not show the aloof ways of many an 'alley cat' or tabby. However, as their manners are typically pleasant and as they seem to enjoy so much of their owner's company and general life, they have claim to be the most perfect of pets. But if you want affection from a cat you must give it in return.

All cats are perfectly capable of making their own living in open country, and they come to man only if they want to do so. A pen-kept Colourpoint that had been forced to change its home and was shut up again for safety managed to escape twice. The first time he lived wild in the woods for two months before being successfully trapped. The second time he escaped for good. By contrast, a Colourpoint carrier returned to the home of her birth after an absence of six years, which started when she was a small kitten. She too had been penned, escaped, and caught again with difficulty. But she recognized her old home, and with evident pleasure, as deduced from the non-stop purring. She was given complete freedom of house and garden and she never strayed, but took her place among the other happy Mingchiu cats, although she would have preferred to have been the only cat. Very slowly, in her middle age, did she learn that it was nice to sit on the lap and have the head stroked. She desperately wanted to live in a house, dashing into the garden at will—she had never been in the garden in her kittenhood. Only when she was brought near an outdoor pen did she voice her disapproval in no uncertain manner.

In other words, whether your Colourpoint loves you or not depends on you. He is prepared to do so, and his whole behaviour will be affected by how you reciprocate, no matter what genes he carries. You can change the colour of his points slightly, for example by changing homes and precipitating a moult, preceding which some dark hairs become pale; you can alter the body colour by indoor climates and lack of light; and you can make or ruin your cat's behaviour patterns by the way you keep him.

Two sleek and hefty well-fed working cats, 'civil servants' with their own maintenance allowance, were peacefully watching the 'telly' in a basement common room one cold and windy evening. An entering superior officer remarked, 'What are you doing here you boys, better go out and do your job on the wharves and in the sheds.' But 'Oh, sir, please let them finish the programme,' pleaded a friend! Actually the subsistence allowance was for one cat, but he brought in a fourfooted pal, to share his dinner and his work, who was allowed to remain, the bipedal civil servants seeing to it that neither of them lacked for anything.

One should not be too anthropomorphic in the interpretation of the behaviour of an animal, but it is equally wrong to consider that an intelligent animal such as a cat has no mentality at all and can thrive in confinement like a greenhouse plant. A cat deprived of all opportunity of choosing its own activities, of doing what it likes, of having 'fun' and interest of its own finding, becomes a neurotic pathetic creature, however hygienic the cage or suitable the food. We all know how a cat will eat what it steals with great gusto, when that same article placed upon its dinner plate would be rejected. It is the same with children and the unripe apples stolen from an orchard. A cat enjoys confinement in a hygienic cage or small pen just as much as a human enjoys a prison cell where there is nothing to do and no access to anything of interest is permitted.

Abroad it is reported that great interest has at times been attracted by Mingchiu cats at shows, because of their charming manners towards humans, and the way in which they greet their owners. The owners of the local cats, all kept in cages, are astonished, never having believed that cats could behave like that. An utterly frustrated cat becomes pathetically uninterested in life, humans and all, and may well become fierce and ready to lash out, not really at any one person, but against its whole manner of miserable enforced life.

It is not enough to keep a cat for its looks, perhaps for its feel, and often for its show-bench potential — unfortunately enormous numbers of cats languish in that manner. And when the cage is unhygienic, dark and uninteresting, their lot is pathetic indeed. In England it is not customary to keep cats in cages, and many persons are unaware of the practice, but even here the ugly head of the cage is being reared and should be firmly suppressed. If you cannot do so without a cage, do not keep a cat at all.

So what does a Colourpoint want, if he is to become a perfect pet? First and foremost he must not be caged, or caused to live in any other type of 'soul-destroying' existence with no scope for his faculties. He can be penned in large and suitable quarters for part of each 24 hours, though he prefers to come and go as he pleases. For safety's sake, he must always be kept in at night. A happy cat does not want to run away, but he must have some freedom at regular intervals.

Cats are not gregarious mammals because of their basically carnivorous diet for which they do not hunt in packs. But they do not like solitary confinement any more than a human does. Two males, friends from kittenhood, will live together peaceably enough for a couple of years, but they usually will fight when fully mature.

The significance of such fighting has been well studied by Dr Ley-hausen[1] together with the meaning of many cat noises. Some barriers must be erected if more than one full male is kept. Units consisting of a family party, with more than one wife to each male, live happily together, a much better arrangement than having solitary males for ever pacing their misery alone in a pen. A male with one or two wives, and freedom for part of their day, will be reasonably content in a well-lit house of about 7 x 5 ft. with plenty of windows, shelves, etc. set in an interesting enclosure of 20 x 14 ft or more. Occasionally the Mingchiu females are allowed to kitten in their own houses along with the other inhabitants. But more usually they come into the human house well beforehand, where the worst restriction that can happen is a closed door at times. Each cat must be made to feel that he is a real pet, and he must feel this even if one of a number in a cattery. No owner can spread personal attentions over too large a number of cats; some twenty adults is an upper limit if other activities are also pursued.

How are the Mingchiu cats treated so that they have the widely acclaimed delightful temperament? Each one is always addressed by name several times a day and each one is given opportunity to indulge in its own particular fad, whatever that may be. Roxana is one of my oldest Colourpoints; she has never been penned. She was spayed at the age of nine years, having been a wonderful breeder. She is my quiet shadow wherever I go. Her face is at the window waiting for my return. She is never demonstrative, but she gives and receives all the time, be it sitting on part of my chair as I work, asking for her front paw to be held, or flopped across my shoulders. She is not a lap cat. She takes a wide stroll of the gardens daily and sleeps on a chair by my bed at night. She enjoys many special privileges which she defends unobtrusively. Her methods are simple towards another trying to take her place. She may just look the other way and move off, but if the usurper tries too often, her eyes flash. She raises her wide and woolly paw, all fingers spread, but not to strike and start a rough house. No, she firmly pushes in the face of the cat that wants to sit on her established spot, and the method works.

[1]Leyhausen, P., 1965, 'The Communal Organization of Solitary Mammals', *Symp. Zool. Soc., Lond.* No. 14, pp. 249-263.

What each cat asks for is usually different, although the general behaviour may be similar. Polo must have his back scratched just so—at one time he had a slightly irritating skin. Zorab must lie on his back for his tummy to be rubbed, four paws in the air; several consider the proper place for a Colourpoint is round the neck. Magog, who detests strangers, and runs and hides when they come, does not like being handled, but she will use her paw vigorously to intercept me if I appear to be passing her by without our customary little private talk, rub of noses and stroke of the head. Along she comes for attention whenever I am near. The boy Choc was always most extravagant in his hugs round the neck in order to lick the face. That formality being over his next attention was the eating of catmint and rolling in it. After that a tour of inspection and sniffing in the garden—the aviaries, he thought, were there for his special entertainment—and finally he had to start a row with some other boy through the netting of some enclosure and try to spray, to register ownership of females belonging to another male. He now lives in another home where he is as free and as happy as he was in the Mingchiu cattery.

The ease with which an adult Colourpoint can change homes depends, not on the detail of his individual genetical make up, but on the manner in which he has lived and the way in which he has been handled. But the inherent difference in temperament between the Siamese and the Colourpoint makes such a change of home easy for the latter if the cat has been suitably treated, in contrast to a pen-kept Colourpoint who ran away for good, both of his penned existences being loveless. Even the most understanding of second owners may be unable to make any headway with an adult Colourpoint that has been unsuitably brought up and whose character is warped for life. By contrast, take Ch. Mingchiu Kamet who left the Mingchiu cattery at the age of $2\frac{1}{2}$ years, strode into his new home, jumped upon laps in a friendly manner, clearly said 'where is my missus', and, the 'liars' that cats are, also said that he had always been in the habit of sitting right in the middle of the dining room table at meal times, although actually he had lived in his own house and enclosure for most of his day and had never been allowed such liberties.

Kittens cannot be treated as individuals to quite the same extent when small because of their numbers but they can never be mass produced. Mingchiu kittens are addressed collectively, but fed separately (Photograph 16); litters are not caged but may be partly restricted to certain rooms. A little of the right kind of attention goes a long way. Simple caging or shutting of doors is usually needed for a few minutes only at meal times, in order to keep the age groups separated, and they all have scope for their own initiatives.

Care must be taken in making an intimate relationship with a cat lest it develop into something so formidable for the cat that it cannot be broken. Some might say formidable for the human too. But let us take just one example. A Siamese cat considered herself to be THE cat of the house; she slept on the bed and sat in the lap the moment there was a lap to sit on. The adored human was her slave. Colourpoints came along, and in increasing numbers, and she was bitterly jealous. She rushed away in a huff when they came near. At the age of eight years she shifted her official home to a house nearby where she was well cared for and realized her dream of being the only cat on the premises, and another became her 'very own human'. But she returned frequently to the original garden, looked at the empty lap at tea time that was hers to take, swore and ran away. Daily she came to the back door and commanded a plate of rabbit, served exactly to her liking, to be eaten out of doors in all weathers. But there were no gentle ways, no gestures of goodwill or friendship. If touched she swore, it was difficult to believe she was still the same cat. Sometimes she came right into the house but she always rushed out again in a rage. She could never in many years resolve the conflict between losing what she once had and the present situation, although she seemed happy enough in her second home, and curiously pleased to see me there if I called. In all she was a pathetic little thing, wanting what she would not take and what was offered to her, a cat of very different basic temperament to the Colourpoint.

VIII THE NEWER COLOURS
Right: Mingchiu Sulafour, a female aged 9 months. She is the first Lilac-pointed Colourpoint to reach championship status with two Challenge Certificates in 1969. The nose is wide and well demarcated, the body cobby and low on the ground, the tail short and full, and the coat long and silky.

IX *Below:* Ch. Mingchiu Ptan, a male Chocolate-pointed Colourpoint aged 3 years who in 1968 became the first Chocolate-pointed champion. He carries Blue and sires Seal, Blue, Chocolate and Lilac-pointed kittens, depending upon his mate.

10. Man-made and natural varieties

It has been stated that a major difference between Birman cats and Colourpoints is that the former are a naturally occurring variety while the latter are man-made. Even the American official classification of domestic varieties of cats has adopted this idea and put it in print. The complete baselessness of this concept, for which not a shred of scientific evidence exists, should now be pointed out.

Let the facts be stated. The Birman cat is said to have turned up in Burma, but with no recorded ancestry, and was imported into France, bred for a number of years and more recently exported to many other countries. The Birman cat in appearance is much like an early Colourpoint in type (see para. 1, p. 31 above), but possesses white feet. The Birman shows the Siamese colour pattern, the coat is not as long as in a typical Longhair, the nose is straight, the ears largish and pricked, and the body lacks the cobby build of a good Longhair. A Birman also turned up from accidental unknown matings in Devon in 1965 and more recently elsewhere in England.

The genes giving the white footed character are widespread in domestic cats but, because the standards adopted for show type varieties has dictated it, the white foot has been eliminated from all our pedigree stocks of such cats. It can be seen often enough in alley cats, and indeed is a frequent colour pattern of many species of domestic animals, such as dogs and horses.

The Birman cat has been synthesized just as surely as has the Colourpoint. In Germany the progeny of a white-footed Siamese and a Longhair ultimately produced Birmans. The breeding was recorded[1] and some of the German Birmans were sent to France for further breeding. Mr B. A. Stirling-Webb and I at one time intended to make a Birman from a white-footed black queen in

[1] R. Wolff, 'Vergessene Leistungen deutscher Züchter: Birma, Khmer und German-Rex', *Die Edelkatze.*, Nürnberg, 1965, **2**, 1–3.

our possession and a wide choice of suitable mates. But his untimely illness and death put a stop to the enterprise, because the Mingchiu cattery was not willing to take in this queen and find the necessary breeding space just to demonstrate that a Birman could be manufactured. However, the demonstration took place under its own steam in Devon. A black-and-white pet of unknown ancestry, purchased in a pet shop, sought her unknown mate in the neighbourhood and produced a Birman among other types of kitten (see above p. 67). The essentials needed for Birman making is the coming together of the genes for Siamese pattern, Longhair and Bicolour, the latter expressing itself as white feet. Not all the white feet at first will have the required gauntlet shape to the white area on the hind legs: that is a refinement. This Devon Birman cat sought her own mate and produced a white-footed Siamese, a Colourpoint and black kittens by the segregation of the type described above. And all this occurred before any Birmans bred in England were distributed.

The chance of a Birman turning up naturally is present wherever Siamese and Bicoloured cats, carrying Longhair, coexist. Birmans may be made more quickly by planned matings, unless the population of freely mating cats is exactly right, as it appeared to be in this part of Devon. A male Siamese cat, not under proper control, and mating with the cats of the neighbourhood, as is the custom of these animals, will inevitably in time lead to the chance appearance of both Colourpoint and Birman cats. If he is a Chocolate-point, other progeny of interest also appear.

Colourpoints as well as Birmans have turned up without the intervention of man, as noted above, and their sudden appearance in places as far apart as Scotland, Devon, Cornwall and Kenya is quite understandable. Colourpoints will continue to turn up accidentally wherever Siamese and Longhair cats coexist, and, as there are probably more plain Longhairs or cats carrying Longhair only than Bicoloured Longhair cats or cats carrying Bicolour and Longhair, the frequency of Colourpoints turning up will be greater than that of Birmans.

There is not the slightest difference scientifically between the mating of a Siamese and a Longhair Blue, for example, which takes place under the watchful eye of a stud owner and a similar mating taking place in the wild when these varieties coexist. And it has been exactly those matings which have been used on at least two occasions for the purpose of ultimately obtaining Colourpoints. It is probable that the cats involved in chance matings will be of not such 'show type' as those whose matings take place under supervision; but the difference, as shown above, between the show-type cats and the others is one of refinement, of the reassortment of genes producing the minor characters which make the show cat what he is.

If further argument is sought upon this subject it should be borne in mind that the first Colourpoint, forming the basis of the pedigrees of a large part of our Colourpoint population today, was one which had no known ancestry and turned up in the wild. Colourpoints and Birmans can both be man-made and they can both be naturally occurring. Whether the American Himalayan cats are exclusively man-made I do not know, but it may be that they are in a nation that cages its Siamese and pedigree cats so carefully. But Himalayan, Colourpoint and Birman will turn up naturally wherever they get the chance.

The enormous amount of scientific work that has been accomplished on the genetics of animals and of the breeding of domestic compared with wild varieties shows that the same basis is common to all. What that basis is in Colourpoints and some other cats has been indicated above; whether they be free or not makes no difference.

There is one major difference between Birmans and Colourpoints. The standard of points adopted for Birmans seeks to maintain the features resembling those of initial crosses between Siamese and Longhair and their descendants, leaving aside the white feet for the moment. The mating of Birman to Birman is like the mating of early Colourpoint to early Colourpoint, and produces no major change. But the standard of points adopted for Colourpoints asks for a cat as like a typical Longhair in type as possible, and thus as time goes on, the Colourpoint becomes less and less like a Birman as its type is improved to approximate more closely to the finest Longhair. This then, and the white feet, are the major differences between Birmans and Colourpoints, not their manner of origin.

11. Housing and habits

The ideal life for a Colourpoint is complete freedom of the owner's house and access by a 'pussflap' or pop-hole to a garden (Photographs 37, 38), or large enclosure, containing plenty of interest to a cat, not to a concrete yard. The owner then may be rewarded with an ideal pet. Colourpoints differ from 'the cat that walked by himself' of Kipling. They are interested in all that goes on in the owner's house and become almost dog-like in their devotion to a particular human. If more than one Colourpoint is kept there may be some jealousy, but they settle down amicably. They like to choose the places where they sit and sleep; they do not like being forced into a routine which is not of their own making, and routines they do make.

Each individual develops his or her own peculiarities, either about the house or garden, or in relation to the owner. There are many derivatives of the rolling behaviour which is normally used by females in display towards a male prior to mating. Ch. Briarry Candytuft is a tremendous roller. She does it when asked, and she expects to be asked several times a day and the rolling must be watched attentively. In the garden she likes to roll to order in particular places, all upon paving. For one week, during my absence, no one asked her to roll. On my return she followed me about wailing, food was spurned, and then I remembered. 'Candy, roll,' I said, and over she went, but over and over again, non-stop right across the kitchen, and she then was evidently satisfied.

Males also roll. Ch. Mingchiu Choc indulged in a daily rolling in one patch of cat mint (*Nepeta*) as soon as he was let out of his own quarters, his fur becoming wet in places with the juices from the bruised plant. After that he went some distance to another cat-mint plant, one in about thirty and always to the same one, here to try to bite the plant to bits at the roots. Ch. Mingchiu Shan, when in his pen, indulges in a curious antic whereby he gets

84

the top of his head as well as all feet on a bench or shelf close to the wire, and he looks up or down at his human friends obliquely. He is clearly disappointed if this gesture is not followed by a reciprocal greeting, by release from his pen or a cuddle. Another male, in his youth and for some years after, liked to get on a roughly horizontal branch of a tree and put his shoulders down on the branch, twisting his body and waving both his front feet in the air as his human friends passed by underneath. Sometimes he nearly fell off in the doing. In middle age he did the same sort of thing on every step of the staircase on the way to bed, together with some rather rough play, also repeated on every step. At the age of approaching eighteen years the old cat still indulged in a slow, very attenuated, 'stairs play' each night. All these activities have their origin in the normal display pattern of the cats' behaviour.

Other performances in relation to the owner vary greatly. One large full-grown male digests his dinner flat on his back with his feet in the air by his master's chair, his flank being supported by the chair leg so that he does not roll over. Saying 'good morning' may be a very extravagant affair, second only to a greeting given at other times in the day following the owner's return from absence. Ch. Mingchiu Souk simply must tidy a beard each morning, paws round master's neck, when she arrives in the bedroom at getting up time. She will leave her kittens in order to go and give this uninvited greeting. And she quietly waits her moment, not hurling herself at the object of her affections, as would a Siamese. Ch. Mingchiu Monique is less patient, and will not be kept waiting for her morning cuddle, inflicting a sharp nip on the leg if the delay is too long. Every cat, if there be more than one, must have individual attention, and of the kind that each appreciates most or has come to expect in their domesticated existence.

The substitute for prey animals such as the rat, mouse or bird, is the basis of much playing with balls of paper, etc. of various sizes, and should form a recognized part of the cat's needs. Even the 'conversation' of the cat with a large or a small bundle of paper in the mouth denotes 'mouse' or 'rat' to those who have analyzed their noises.

A recognized scratching post, accepted by both cat and owner,

85

is a need in the house. A table leg with a piece of old carpet wrapped round it serves the purpose most adequately, particularly when the floor is carpeted. A scratch post on a shiny floor is not so favoured because the back feet slip. The old carpet round the leg gets torn to shreds and needs frequent renewal, but the cats soon learn that they are allowed to scratch there. This is a must, even when there is access to a garden, and the cat's claws are thereby kept in order. There is no need to clip the claws of a well-kept cat except in extreme old age. To avoid all friction on the subject of clawed upholstery, soft furnishings covered by the material called 'Vynair' made by I.C.I., or other such fabric, provides the complete answer. No claws will penetrate the material and so the cats derive no pleasure or usefulness from trying to claw it, the coverings remain intact indefinitely, and the 'scratch pole' is triumphant.

A tray of peat moss, or any of the other absorbent cat litters on the market, is usually useful, and essential if there are kittens. For adult cats the tray must not be too small, at least 16–18 inches long. If the tray has no 'legs', four pieces of lino, or other such substance, about the size of a penny, can be stuck under the corners, so that the main part of the tray is advantageously kept off the floor.

The cats should be provided with their own baskets, boxes, blankets, etc. for sleeping, and the surroundings must be draught free. The latter is most important for kittens, even with their long hair. They catch cold very easily. A simple low screen around a sleeping place is often very useful in cold weather. Adult Colourpoints can exist without artificial heat in winter in England, but do better with a little heat as described below. If kept indoors under conditions of much winter heat and dryness of atmosphere, no fine coat may develop.

A Colourpoint appreciates access to a garden which is full of interesting smells, with grass, flower beds, paths and trees to climb. And they enjoy running the whole length of a garden, so obtaining exercise which they cannot get in an enclosure of the order of about 20 feet in length or in the house. Dig they will in the flower beds, but unless the cats are many, the destruction caused is not usually great. Walls to walk along are always popular, since cats do not like crossing wide-open spaces. But if the garden leads easily to a road, something must be done for the cats' protection, since modern roads take a very heavy toll of cats. Wiring off a garden from a road is necessary; something can sometimes be done about front gardens, by giving a cat a fright there with a large borrowed dog, so that the visit is not repeated. But if the Colourpoint shares the home with a dog this experiment will not work.

Some female Colourpoints will be content to remain within the confines of a fair-sized garden, and at first the males may be the same, but sooner or later they go exploring into other gardens. There may be no harm in this, depending upon the neighbourhood, but more often this wandering needs to be curbed. However, it is a normal activity for the cat, and Colourpoints, although much more stop at home than 'alley' cats, show the same sort of social and territorial behaviour described by Dr P. Leyhausen[1] for domestic cats in general. A resident male is a great deterrent to wandering by a female, which is usually undertaken prior to a calling period and serves to scout out the local males.

Colourpoints readily learn what they are and are not allowed to do in their owner's house. But cats lack the human concept of honesty. They will steal what they know they are not supposed to have, right under the owner's nose, desisting at once when spoken to. They will behave properly in the dining room at meal times in the owner's presence, but when he is out they may sit in the middle of the table and claim it as their right, as if it was an established custom. Some individuals learn to do the most unnatural things, such as sitting up and begging for food like a dog, but they will only do it when it pleases them, not necessarily when it pleases the owner. A pair of cats each knew how to beg at the order 'sit'. The female would never beg for her dinner—the boy could beg for two. But after dinner she would always beg to order, and at first was rewarded with a saucer of coffee milk; he would not beg then. In later years she would still beg when she didn't want the milk and refused it. The begging ensured a bit of personal attention.

The owner has a multitude of ways in which he can indicate to the cat his displeasure at any particular action, provided he does it at once. The cat, who expects a lot from his owner, has much more limited means of conveying displeasure, but there is one very

[1]Leyhausen, P., 1965, 'The Communal Organization of Solitary Mammals', *Symp. Zool. Soc. Lond.* No. 14, pp. 249–263.

strong retaliation which is at times meted out. Very, very rarely, but on more than one occasion and by two of my cats, intense displeasure has been registered about my going out in the evening, and on my return hastily serving drinks etc. to visitors without a word to cats. The injured party has mounted the settee beside me, turned her rear, and deliberately soaked me to the skin, an act of supreme jealousy which is certain to produce instant reaction, although not of a favourable nature for the cat! These two cats normally have been meticulously clean in their habits about the house. When all else fails this is the type of behaviour they can fall back on.

Up to the age of two years a male can easily be kept in the owner's home, whether he becomes sexually mature at 13 months or two years. But after that he will spray, which indicates a registering of ownership of his surroundings and is impossible to stop. Some males are far more unpleasant than others, one cannot tell in advance what is ahead. If the male is to be a house pet he should be neutered under a year in age before he starts this sort of thing. If he is required for breeding, then he must have his own quarters. He need not live in them all the time, he needs his freedom to do what he likes for part of each day, and he prefers not to live alone. He will settle down happily with two or three wives, all being given some freedom.

The type of housing which is suitable depends in part on the climate. Premises which are satisfactory for the British Isles will not do at all for countries where the winter temperatures go below zero. In the Mingchiu cattery in England each mature stud cat has his own house, a prefabricated workshop, 5 × 7 feet with windows on three sides, a gently sloping roof, not a gable, and a door with a pop hole (Photographs 39–41). The house stands in an enclosure of at least 14 × 20 feet, the wire (plastic covered 2-inch chain link netting except where there are kittens) passes about 18 inches above the roof, so that the cats can sit there, a pleasure they much enjoy (Photographs 42, 43). Larger runs are desirable where space allows.

About 100 feet of floor boards per house and run provides shelves inside the house and outside, at different levels, for the cats to walk about on. A peat bunker in the house serves also as a seat for use when grooming the cats. The walls are covered with polystyrene insulation sheets and are faced with an adhesive plastic for

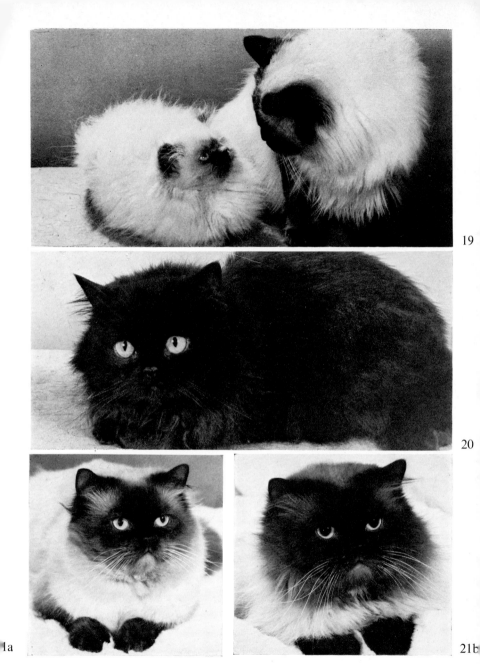

19

20

1a

21b

IN PURSUIT OF TYPE
Above: Two Mingchiu winners on different occasions of best Longhair kitten in show, Blue-point left and Seal-point right. *Middle:* Champion Mingchiu Magog, unbeaten on the show bench by any Black Longhair cat or kitten. She is an invaluable Longhair Black carrier of the Colourpoint pattern, which she transmits to half her offspring. *Below:* Gr. Ch. Mingchiu Murdock of Badi, a Seal-point male aged 14 months, left, and 26 months, right, where his mask is fully developed and includes the chin (cf. Photographs 1a, b). He was highest scoring Seal-point male and BOX Himalayan for the Southern U.S. Region 1968-9.

Left: Ch. Mingchiu Monique, a Blue-point female in summer coat at 8 months, ears pricked to the bright lights.

Right, above: Mingchiu Karelia, Blue-point, at 3½ months, showing short, well-demarcated nose, wide top of head, small, well-directed ears, wide muzzle, and very long coat. She was best longhair kitten in show, Ellesmere Port 1968. *Below:* Ch. Mingchiu Polo at 4 years showing flowing coat, fine profile with firm chin, well-demarcated short nose and small ears.

23

24

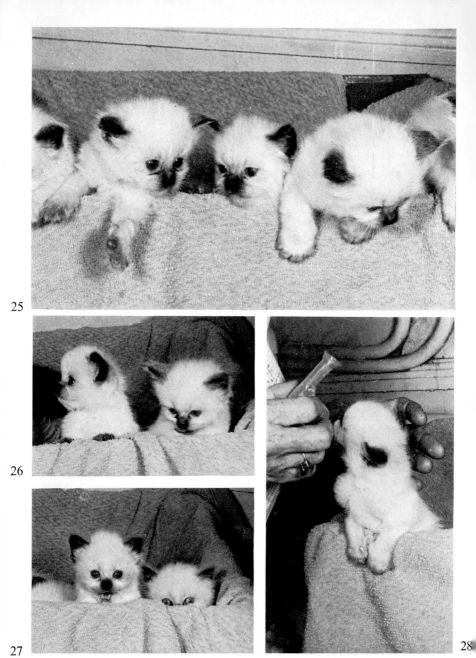

25

26

27

28

KITTENS AND BOTTLE FEEDING
Left: 4-week-old Mingchiu kittens needing supplementary feeding. They are waking up and screaming for their bottle. They cannot yet climb out of their box. See also Photograph 30 opposite p. 104.

ease of cleaning. The ceiling is lined with insulating sheets. Two wide shelves are built one above another, with a 2-foot thermostatically controlled tubular heater under the lower shelf. Shutters can in part close in the lower shelf, so that, if required, a constant temperature of 60 degrees can be maintained on this shelf in cold weather, a necessity if kittens are to be born in the house. Usually kittens are born in my own house and not in the garden. The slight heating of the stud house keeps it dry, and usually the general temperature is maintained only a little above that of the outside, the door being widely open all the time in summer and the pop hole open day and night in winter. The doors, however, face away from the prevailing wind. The outside temperatures seldom fall below 10–15 degrees F. The floor covering must be hard and smooth so that it is easily cleaned. One upper window of the house is usually always open, at least a little, and shelves run along the lower level of the glass of the lower windows so that the cats can sit on them and look out. There is about 9 feet of such window benching in each house giving plenty of choice in roosting places.

The prefabricated 'workshops' forming the houses of the Mingchiu cattery have been erected in pairs, mirror images of each other, with doors facing in the same direction, away from the prevailing winds. A gap of at least 6 feet lies between each pair which is roofed by a curved dome of translucent plastic, such as 'corroglase' (Photograph 39, right). The open ends of this intervening space are completed with walls fore and aft, a floor and a door of the same materials as the houses, one side wall of each house becoming a party wall limiting a third middle house or shed. The central curved roof passes insensibly into the sloping roofs of the houses on either side, giving a much pleasanter general appearance than that of separate houses, each unit of three being so very much wider than it is high.

Each run contains a plot of grass, some paving made with 'Kentstone' or other tiling, set in pebbles and sand and close together, so that draining is rapid and efficient after rain and the area does not puddle. No cement is used here. Natural and artificial trees are included. Cats particularly like individual seats well off the ground, the top of a small stepladder is always popular, or the top of a cut tree trunk. Tiles such as used for paving, 18 inches square, make decorative and very popular 'tables' when set on a couple of decorative cement wall units about 15 inches square, acting as legs. Both the top and the space under the table for hiding and shade, are used by the cats (Colour photographs V, XV, Photograph 42). Large tree trunks and branches are provided for scratching, walking about on and for the amusement of kittens. In a corner where the sun falls is a bed of catmint (*Nepeta*), wired in (Photograph 43 right), so that the cats can chew the parts that grow through and do not destroy the whole plants. A peat moss tray is provided both inside the house and outside in the run under a permanent shelter from rain, which is also a bench (Photograph 42 left). The ground here is concrete for ease of cleaning, and a concrete border to the pen of about 15 inches in width lies at the base of the fencing, because it is in these positions that the cats are most apt to soil their surroundings. Grass they enjoy in the summer, it is cool and amusing to lie in, etc., but they do not respect it, and unless the enclosure is very large indeed it is not practicable to have much of the pen under grass. The surround to the house must be hard, and concrete should lie under the house also, and so prevent tunnelling by rats and mice from the outside into this nice dry area.

The lower 3 feet of the fencing should be opaque on the windward side and this may also serve to give shade in summer. Benches are provided on either side of each run which are in shade either morning or evening. Where there are adjacent pens the party fence is opaque on the lower 3 feet, and above this the shelves in the two pens are not at the same levels, or squabbles between the males would follow. Springs on the gates to the runs are easily made from the double-hooked elastic ropes used for attaching luggage to carriers.

A permanent garden table near the gates, with a stone top, large enough to take a tray of plates, is of great service. Flower beds surround the pens, *Nepeta* and other flowers forming a bank outside the run wires, which in summer stops most of the bickering between male cats free in the garden and those in pens. A collection of different varieties of clematis climb the fencing on the outside, providing shade for the cats and interest for the observer, being planted so that their roots are in shade (covered by slabs of stone) and their foliage in full sun. Flower beds of a more extensive kind separate the groups of pens, and the whole, with a lawn and the aviaries of foreign birds, forms as spectacular and pleasant a small garden as anyone might wish to have. In fact it attracts visitors from across all the oceans, but unfortunately the cats are in full bloom when the flowers are not.

The Mingchiu cattery does not take in calling queens for mating, and accommodation for this purpose therefore is not needed. The cats live very happily in small family parties, but if all the girls are removed for kittening and the male is left in sole possession, he voices his displeasure in no uncertain manner. He does not like living alone. If mating facilities are wanted for visitors, then some shut-in quarter for the visitor must be provided so that she can make friends with the male through the wires before they are put together. The reigning females must, of course, be removed, or must live elsewhere. The accommodation just described provides ample benching at a suitable height for the male to make his escape from the female after mating if need be.

There are many catteries with good accommodation, constructed on different plans and out of different materials, but the essentials are common to all. The principal faults of much housing for cats advertised in print and exhibited at shows are their smallness in size, the roofs are gabled and the cats have no access to them, the benching is quite inadequate to provide sufficient variety and interest to a cat, the interior is too dark, and far too little thought is given to providing interest in the run which is too small.

91

12. Food and maintenance

As with housing, so with food: there is a great variety of suitable ways of feeding cats, depending upon the available foodstuffs, but the essential food values are common to all diets. An adult cat needs two substantial meals a day and usually a milky mix as well. Neuter cats often prefer to have only one meal a day. Pregnant and nursing queens need at least three good meals a day and a milky mix. Kittens, when first completely weaned, need five meals a day, and the number should be reduced to four and three as the age increases. Too much feeding with insufficient times between meals can be as bad as too little. Some adult cats dislike anything containing milk. All drink water in considerable quantities, and water should be available at all times.

Meat forms the principal component of the cats' diet, and preferably in the form of small whole mammals. Usually this presents difficulties and must be supplemented by lean meat from larger animals, and it should be remembered that such meat is deficient in a number of essentials present in a natural diet where bones, blood, brain, liver, etc., are also eaten. Fish should only form a small part of the menu and offals such as leitz (lung), heart, melts (spleen) should not form a substantial part of the food and are better excluded. Giblets are unsuitable, even prepared gizzards. Food supplements in the form of added vitamins, A and D from Halibut liver oil (or Adexolin); Brewer's yeast in powder form, or Kitzyme tablets, provide ample vitamins of the B complex as well as proteins and minerals, the former being the less expensive. Milk, oat products, glucose, hard foods of some kind (e.g. Seanip, Purina Co.) and bones to chew will ensure a cat in perfect condition. Eggs, particularly egg white in kitten feeding, can take their place in the food. But every cat will not accept the same foods, they have marked individual preferences, and are prepared to starve rather than eat what they do not like, however suitable the food value may be. It is no use laying down the law about food, the cat's likes and dislikes must be catered for.

Few cats thrive on plenty of fish. Although some do so, others living on such a diet will suffer from skin disorders and loss of coat on the underside, which can be rectified if fish is withheld. Carbohydrates and vegetables are not readily digested and should not form a substantial part of the diet, because the cat cannot produce the appropriate digestive enzymes.

The eating of grass practised by most cats, particularly early in the morning, possibly has some food value, but a service it clearly renders is promoting a vomit, which gets rid of the hair swallowed by the cats' grooming activities and leaves the stomach ready for breakfast. Not all cats eat grass, and those that do not are quite healthy. They cough up their fur balls usually with ease.

As much variety as possible should be provided in the food, and if a mixture of food is given at one meal it is better not mushed up so that every mouthful is the same. Raw meat once a day is strongly recommended and it is better not minced fine. Larger pieces, preferably of the dimensions of earthworms, give the teeth something to do, and too large portions are not swallowed which will produce indigestion. For kittens the meat is suitably cut to matchstick proportions for 9–10-week-olds and onwards, but younger kittens need the meat more finely cut and free from connective tissue; this is most easily prepared by 'scraping'. A sharp knife is scraped across a lean piece of meat, semi-frozen for choice, and only the fine material so scraped off is given to the kittens. The indigestible connective tissue, which may be abundant within the meat, is left behind on the chunk.

The preparation of raw meat for a number of cats is most easily done with a hand or electrically driven slicing machine which slices the meat at any required thickness such as those made by Ritter. For a small number of animals a sharp knife on a wooden board is sufficient. All raw meat should be kept in the freezing compartment of a fridge or in a deep freezer and taken out just as required. Meat already minced needs to be eaten at once, and only uncut meat should be stored for more than a few hours. Meat should always be packed in polythene bags in a fridge to retain its moisture and prevent needless frosting up of the fridge.

93

Cooked meat, hares, rabbits, etc., should be thoroughly well cooked until quite tender, either in closed containers in the oven (3 hours) or on a gas or electric 'ring', or more conveniently in a pressure cooker for 30–60 minutes at 15 pounds pressure. The water, added before cooking, forms a rich jelly or stock containing valuable solutes which can all be used up in the food, mainly as a basis instead of water, for making porridge for breakfast out of Quick Quaker Oats. The porridge should be thin in consistency, cats do not like it stiff.

The most useful milk mixtures for adults, given either at mid-day in between the main meals or at bed time, contain milk, glucose, and either Scott's Midlothian Oat Food (M.O.F.) or Farex or raw egg. Glucose, to the measure of a heaped dessert-spoonful per pint of milk mix, is sufficient; too much is to be care-fully avoided. The M.O.F. is preferred because it stimulates fine coat growth in Colourpoints; a level dessertspoonful per pint of milk is made up according to the directions on the packet. Similarly Farex can be used or a whole beaten up egg. It should be remem-bered that plain cow's milk is often indigestible to cats and should not be given. The addition of egg white to milk eases the digestion of the latter. Since each cat needs only a tablespoon of milk mix, the quantity made up will depend upon the number of cats.

For kittens an ideal milk mix, which can be used also for bottle feeding from birth, is made up as follows: Boil a large cup, and the business end of a spoon and fork in a saucepan of water. Take out the cup with the spoon and as cleanly as possible crack an egg and tip the white into the cup. The yolk can be added to adults' breakfast porridge. Lightly whisk the egg white with the sterilized fork and add to it boiled milk that has cooled somewhat, other-wise the egg white will set. Fill the cup brim full, adding also a tea-spoonful of glucose. Cover, and keep in the fridge, warming up small quantities as required. If this milk mix is used for bottle feed-ing, remove some of it with the boiled spoon and fill the feeding bottle, which has previously been sterilized by boiling or by some other method. Do not return any unused mix to the main supply in the cup. Let adults or large kittens finish up any left overs. Com-plan may be used as part of the milk mix. The American product Esbilac (The Borden Chemical Co.) seems to be ideal for kittens.

Milk mixtures are essential to kittens and very good for all adults that will take them, but it should be remembered that too much will invariably lead to indigestion. A nursing queen can take perhaps three dessertspoonfuls per day instead of the normal two, depending on the queen; more may cause diarrhoea. Sometimes when a nursing queen is very keen to drink milk it is better to give her the baby's egg white mix described above, with or without a larger amount of egg white, rather than the normal adult mix. The egg white will ease digestion, but sterilizing utensils etc, need not be practised.

The conversion of basic feeding principles into a diet sheet is open to endless variations in detail. The diet of the adult Mingchiu cats is as follows, the quantities given being for one cat, but even this is very variable, depending on size, age and whether the cat is breeding or not.

Breakfast   2 dessertspoonfuls of porridge made with the stock from cooking the meat of the day before (see above), and about $2\frac{1}{2}$ oz. or more of raw cut up lean meat (whale, horse, beef, cow or kangaroo beef), a little cooked, sliced horse liver, and a little Saval 1 (a puppy biscuit) crumbled on top, 4 drops of halibut liver oil or Adexolin (Glaxo Laboratories). Two cats with a tendency towards constipation have a little Allbran crumbled into the food instead of Saval, or a teaspoonful of Isogel (Allen & Hanbury) every other day. One cat dislikes porridge and has plain meat, another has plain cooked rabbit, but most of them enjoy the porridge. All foods are served warm.

2 p.m.   2 dessertspoonfuls of the M.O.F. milk mix served warm.

5–6 p.m. meal   Cooked meats (usually hare, rabbit or beef), as much as they will eat, with a small quantity of cooked fish, 4 drops of halibut liver oil and a dusting of Brewer's yeast. Seanip (Purina Co.) and/or Felix (Felix Catfood Ltd., Biggleswade, Beds.) is put out in separate dishes.

95

10 p.m.　　　　For nursing and expectant queens, any of the above foods that they like, but no more milk.

Cats need a certain amount of fat in the diet, but they cannot assimilate much of it from fat meat, and most of their meat is better lean.

A neuter cat does well on at least 4 drops of halibut liver oil per day in most climates, but more is desirable if the season, or the climate, is particularly sunless. More is always desirable when breeding. When there has been too little vitamins A and D in the mother's food kittens may be born with kinked tails or cleft palates, no genetical kink being present in the breeding stock. At least 6 to 8 drops of halibut liver oil per day is a satisfactory addition to the food of breeding females and 3 or 4 drops of this oil, or Adexolin, twice daily, for kittens in the English climate. A good demonstration of the efficacy of added vitamins A and D as a protection against some diseases was provided during an epidemic of rhinotracheitis in London. Some 25 adult Minchiu cats had been taking a regular 4 drops of halibut liver oil daily and did not contract the disease, a killer in the neighbourhood at that time. One neuter male, who always fed alone, had only 1 to 2 drops of the oil daily and he was ill for 3 weeks with the disease. Also six kittens aged 3 to 7 months had received only 1 drop of oil per day and all contracted the disease, some seriously. A kitten, aged 6 months, had been given adexolin or halibut liver oil twice a day since the age of 3 weeks, for another reason, and he remained healthy. Two litters of kittens aged 4 to 5 weeks contracted the disease, but another litter in the same room, given Adexolin twice a day from the age of 3 weeks, did not. Clearly a desirable dose for weaned kittens is 3 to 4 drops twice daily in the English climate and if infections are known to be about; and unweaned kittens of 3 weeks onwards can be protected by 1 to 2 drops twice per day, a very worthwhile precaution.

A sufficiency of hard or raw food is necessary to keep the teeth in order. Most but not all Colourpoints will take some Felix or Seanip daily and other more expensive foods of this kind are available. A few have a passion for eating raw whiting, starting from the tail, a kind of fish much preferred to other sorts of

X PROGRESS
Above: An early Colourpoint with a fine frill and good blue eyes, which are so easy to obtain combined with much too long and straight a nose.
XI *Below*: Ch. Mingchiu Mudoba showing all features of a good type Colourpoint.

sea fish. A small fish, raw, or a lesser portion of a larger fish, eaten once or twice a week keeps the teeth in perfect condition. Bones to chew at from the joints cooked for human meals are always popular, and again suffice to preserve the teeth. Cats living entirely on soft foods soon acquire disordered mouths which lead to decay, cancer and endless troubles. But until kittens have grown their permanent teeth, and have shed their milk dentition, they are not capable of eating as much hard or raw food as the adults, and may get indigestion from swallowing too large pieces of meat. However, large chunks of meat to chew are useful, even if the kittens do not swallow much of it. If a cat's gums show a red line along the base of the teeth, hydrogen peroxide, diluted one part in ten, brushed on with a soft brush daily for a few days, may cure the condition, which should then be followed with some improvement in the diet.

For cats as well as humans, a diet that suits one individual perfectly may not be so suitable for another. A tendency towards constipation can be dealt with by mixing some Allbran into the food; this step is not welcomed by the cat and must be done with discretion. A dessertspoonful a day is a great help and can be crumbled into the breakfast porridge instead of cat biscuit (Saval 1). A little liquid paraffin at night is also useful, given by a large polythene pipette or more easily just added to the meal; or Isogel may be used, see above. A cat with an unpleasant breath can be improved by half a tablet of milk of magnesia at bedtime, or a smear of the fluid preparation put on the nose to be licked off. One Mingchiu stud cat was habitually too thin in the body, and had an easily irritated skin and harsh coat. Three months of half a tablet of milk of magnesia at bedtime transformed him, and the treatment has been repeated occasionally. His skin and coat are as they should be and his frame is well covered.

Cats and kittens when moving homes are sometimes put off their food by the change and may refuse to eat for days. The worried new owner wonders what to do with an animal that will not eat any of the things that it is said to have been having. It is worth putting on record that few cats can resist a kipper, even if they have never tasted one before, and some have broken their fast upon tinned tuna. Once food has been taken, then the menu can be varied, and normal feeding soon established. One five-month-old

Colourpoint broke a five-day fast upon smoked salmon, and after that it was plain sailing! The feeding of kittens is further considered on p. 118.

Coats need attention, particularly when moulting. Then it is desirable to put a coarse comb or plastic brush through the coat daily to remove the loose hairs. Otherwise dense hard felts of fur form close to the skin which are difficult to remove. For most of the year a Colourpoint largely looks after its own coat, but grooming is always desirable, although not a daily necessity.

Dusting the coat fortnightly, or when required, with G-Hex (McDermott Chemicals Ltd., Runcorn, Cheshire, England) is a very easy way of controlling fleas effectively in summer. This is a very important matter, because cats can bring in many unwanted passengers when they go for walks, and the eating of an infected flea leads to tape worm. I find this preparation far more efficient than any of the more easily obtainable advertised products. Whether the flea is infected or not depends upon the neighbourhood; in some places every flea is a danger, but in others this is not so. Banks of ivy, in which cats push their way after birds and mice, and sometimes long dry grass are a menace in harbouring fleas. These can hatch out when the vibration of the cat's presence reaches the pupa, in which stage the parasite can rest for years on end. Brushing a coat free from the marks left by fleas should be done and all brushings should be cleanly removed afterwards, because flea larvae feed on just this material, made from the cat's blood by the fleas. The presence of a tapeworm is evident from the rice-like white segments of the worm which adhere to the outside of the faeces. Treatment is best done by either of the preparations: Cestarsol (May & Baker Ltd, Dagenham, Essex) or Scolaban (Burroughs, Wellcome & Co.); the latter causes no reaction by the cat and can be used on pregnant females, but only adult cats of 12 months and over can be treated with either of these cures. Infections in kittens are much more difficult to deal with and your veterinary surgeon should be consulted. Treatment for roundworms is much easier and there are many suitable products on the market.

The beautiful powder-puff coat of the show cat, in which every hair stands away from every other, is easily obtained by using Johnson's Baby Powder, or some similar relatively scentless talcum powder. Sprinkling the powder into the coat once a day for six days, and on the seventh day brushing out well, gives the desired effect. Particular attention should be given to the most greasy parts of the coat, behind the ears, and in males the top few inches at the base of the tail. The heavy grease on the tail is best removed by applying plenty of Fuller's earth, brushing out the next day as far as possible, and repeating the process daily until the fur is perfectly clean and a fine fluffy brush decorates the cat. If you are on good terms with your cat none of this grooming presents any problem, many of them enjoy it very much. But there are a few who dislike talcum powder intensely; it makes them salivate and they become miserable. Fuller's earth (Rouse Bros. Ltd., London W.1) can be used for the whole coat in such cases. The type of brush or comb matters a lot. Except during moulting, when loose fur must be taken out, a comb should be sparingly employed. A brush with coarse flexible plastic teeth is much better, because it does not destroy the coat. There is no need to bath a Colourpoint. They all hate getting wet, although sitting about in the rain is often not objected to, because the thick pelt in winter keeps the skin dry, even in the rain.

Cats swallow some of their coat when doing their own toilet, and this fur is normally vomited up with no difficulty. But when heavily moulting the fur ball may be massive. If the cat goes off its food at such a time the fur inside may be causing trouble, and a dessertspoonful of liquid paraffin at bed time, for one or two nights, usually relieves the condition.

Ears must be kept clean, preferably with lotion obtained from a veterinary surgeon. Infection from other cats with ear mites is readily acquired, and spreads rapidly from one cat to another. Treatment with Otodex (Strenol Products Ltd, 240 Earls Court Road, London, S.W.5) is the most easy and effective, and it is best applied from a pipette, not more than 3 or 4 drops being put well into the ear. If more is used it does not hasten the cure but marks the coat until the next moult. Treatment for 4 days is sufficient, following the instructions on the bottle. No cleaning is required. Slight fur stains made by using too much Otodex may not be apparent in daylight, but show up extremely under strip lighting, such as sometimes used to illuminate show halls.

99

It is not infrequent that even the best kept cats need to take a pill or capsule prescribed by a veterinary surgeon. It is not usually difficult to administer a pill if you do it correctly and quickly. Otherwise the cat may resist so strongly that the situation becomes very distressing. Go to the cat when he suspects nothing and turn his nose upwards by putting your hand over the top of his head. Quickly lower his jaw, with the other hand if need be, and drop the pill exactly down the throat, shut the mouth, holding it shut for a moment. If your aim has been good, he will swallow the pill and forget about it. But if the aim has not been good he will twist his tongue until he spits out the offending pill. A second attempt, if needed, meets with greater resistance than the first. A cat sitting in the unfamiliar surroundings of the veterinary surgeon's surgery will behave perfectly, when at home he may fight and resist. When a cat deliberately regurgitates the pill, after you think that it has been truly swallowed, you may push the pill quickly past recall with the tip of your little finger.

But if in real difficulty make a simple 'pill pusher' out of a piece of polythene tubing, about $\frac{1}{4}$-inch diameter; a $3\frac{1}{2}$–4-inch length is sufficient. Make a cut at one end for about $\frac{1}{4}$–$\frac{1}{3}$-inch on two sides of the tube, so that pills of different sizes can be pushed into the open end and stick there. Have a rod of polythene which loosely fits into the tube and is about half an inch longer. A drawing pin can be fixed into the end of the rod, forming a convenient knob. The 'rod' can be made from tubing of the right size, with the end solidified by heat from a small flame. Plunging the rod fully into the tube will push out the pill inserted into the split end. So charge the 'pusher', open the cat's mouth, not very wide is enough, hold the tube between first and second fingers, and quickly put the pill end into the throat; push the knob with the thumb, and withdraw the tube. The job is done and the pill delivered past recall in a moment and before the cat realizes what has happened. With this simple instrument I once delivered capsules of Penbritin to 57 strange cats in 43 minutes, including walking considerable distances about a cattery to reach the cats; the owner's estimate for the job was many hours and much blood spilt. Get someone to hold a cat for you, if you like, while you manipulate the 'pusher'. A cat breeder has good use for a pill pusher of this type, a polythene pipette and perhaps a glass kitten feeding bottle, all of which are easy to come by and easy to clean.

If in further difficulty with the administration of a prescribed medicine, wrap the cat or kitten in a towel first, the head projecting. This impedes unco-operative movement, mainly because widespread sensory stimulation of the hairs of the cat is thus effected. A cat wearing a wide cylinder of paper round the middle will often fall down and seem unable to walk because of this stimulation.

Cattery housing and runs need to be kept very clean. Besides washing and sweeping, the floors, walls, paving, etc. need regular wiping or sponging down with disinfectants after they have been cleaned in the ordinary manner. Care must be exercised in the choice of disinfectant, since those containing phenols are unsuitable for the cat's feet. Izal (Izal Ltd., Thorncliffe, Sheffield) is cheap and effective, but leaves the surfaces slightly sticky, unless wiped again. Benzalkonium chloride leaves no stickiness, a 1 per cent solution known as 'Roccal' is ready for use and the relatively cheaper 10 per cent solution of Benzalkonium chloride can be diluted (Berk Pharmaceuticals Ltd, Godalming, Surrey). In summer all crevices in houses and runs, the grass, etc can be sprayed with 'Lindane Dust', 'G-Hex' or other Gammexane containing preparation, about 0·6 per cent, in order to control fleas, ticks, etc. The use of a 'Gammexane smoke generator No. 22' (Imperial Chemical Industries Ltd) is recommended as needed for insect control in animal houses.

After infectious disorders, both viral and bacterial, it is essential to use more drastic measures. Normal cleaning finished, all surfaces can be wiped with Lysol and then wiped again with clean water. Fumigation of a room or house for cats with formaldehyde vapour is easily and effectively achieved. The room must be well closed, and about 100 cc ($\frac{1}{4}$ cupful) of 40 per cent formaldehyde is poured over about 100 gm (1 oz) of potassium permanganate crystals placed in a metal container and standing upon something which is heat resistant. Leave the room shut until the following day. If some cats but not others have an infection, all feeding plates can be rinsed in 1 per cent Benzalkonium chloride (Roccal) and left to drain and drip dry. To do this at all times is a wise precaution since it prevents spread of infections by the plates.

13. Breeding and general management

If you have a Colourpoint female and wish to breed from her, you should appreciate that it is an exacting job which must be done properly. It is no use thinking that you will have a queen and just breed from her occasionally when it happens to suit you. You must either breed from her properly, when she wants to breed, or have her spayed and kept as a pet. There is no intermediate road which spells either health or happiness for the cat. If you decide to breed you must also decide on how you are going to obtain a mating unless you have your own male. Successful breeding is very much easier if you keep a breeding pair of cats. If your queen must travel even a small distance to visit a suitable stud, the chances of obtaining a successful mating at the first attempt are slight. The queen may go off call because of the journey, or because of the strange surroundings. She may not like the male, she may be frightened and huddle in a corner for days, she may be furious and attack the strange boy and drive him away, so that he is intimidated, only to resume her yelling when she gets home. One may have to try on half a dozen successive calls before achieving a successful mating, or one may be lucky at the first attempt. And continual calling without successful mating does the cat no good. She does not eat well and possibly ovarian cysts, which prevent future breeding, may be formed in this manner.

A Colourpoint may call (come into season) as early as 8 months and successfully rear her family, but it is much better for her to be mated later. It is unusual to call so young, but Ch. Mingchiu Mopette did it, and I helped her with the feeding of the kittens. And Mingchiu Danladi (Self-chocolate Longhair) most competently raised a litter of 5 when she was only 10 months old herself. But breeding at over a year in age is usually better. Breeding young may result in kittens but no milk. However, when this happens usually all goes well at the next litter. The increase in the intensity of light and in the length of day are the main stimulants to breeding, and most females will call in January to March in England. If they reach the age of a year in the autumn they usually do not call until early the following year, but if they are 11 months old in February they are likely to call. Good breeding females sometimes do not begin until nearly two years of age. Breeding may take place at any time of the year.

Male Colourpoints usually take longer to become mature than females. Rarely a stud will sire at 13 months or younger, usually he is much older, and he may not be useful until two years of age. But the slowness in reaching maturity does not indicate future inefficiency as a stud. Every male I have raised and kept for my own use has proved to be an efficient and reliable stud. Most of the Mingchiu females are good breeders also, but I have had a few females who produce more kittens than they can rear without getting thin or receiving help in the way of supplementary feeding. Only two females in the Mingchiu cattery have not succeeded in breeding, out of the many Colourpoints produced over ten years.

The success of breeding, and its frequency, depends in large measure on the health and happiness of the cats. Several Mingchiu queens produce three litters a year and thrive on it, others produce only two or one. The number of kittens in a litter is usually smaller than in Siamese. It is also variable, two to four being the most usual numbers. Less frequent are the litters of five or six. I have had one litter of nine, all of which were reared, three by the mother and six were bottle fed, changing round the three daily. Thereby the mother remained in nice condition by the time the kittens were fully weaned on to plate feeding.

Successful breeding, without kitten losses, depends also on how much the cats trust and care for their owner. Most of my queens like me to be near them at kittening. Two habitually fetch me for the event. It is necessary to give a little attention and often. One of my oldest Colourpoints lost only three of her sixty-three kittens. One was too large and was born dead, and twice she accidentally nipped the kitten's tummy when eating the cord. I saw to it that she did not do this again, by putting my hand round each new born kitten until she had finished eating the placenta. But the

103

owner must not do anything which the cat regards as interference. It is necessary to be sure that the kittens are being fed adequately and if not they must be bottle fed or a foster mother found. Very rarely is the latter necessary, but I have had one excellent breeder who never came into milk fully until near the end of the first week. The litters all thrived on 5 bottle-feeds the first day, 4 the second, 3 the third, and so on until the mother took over entirely. The owner must also learn to understand what a cat wishes to impart. A queen may come along crying, or tail wagging, or she may dump a kitten at my feet. It may mean her box is too hot, or too cold, or too this, or too that, or that she has not enough milk, and it is up to the owner to understand and act upon it. If everything is going well it is self evident, and the kittens will be silent except when disturbed by their mother's comings and goings.

If more than one Colourpoint is kept for breeding, there are advantages in that one female can help another with too little milk, so that the owner does not have to supplementary feed. Mingchiu Snuff produced her first litter with no trouble, but she had no milk. Her kittening box was in the same room as that of Mingchiu Trivia, who had kittens a week older. Trivia listened to the hungry wails of the newborns until she could bear it no longer. Quietly she crept out of her box, took Snuff's kittens one by one out of their box, added them to her own and fed them. Snuff did not mind. I provided them with one very large box for the two litters and the mums joined forces. Trivia did most of the feeding while Snuff did the washing and baby sitting. The combine worked excellently.

Usually it is better to keep the litters quite separate, or there may be a lot of baby snatching, and far too many kittens will find their way into certain boxes and endless stealing will go on. Most queens have a complex about bigger and better babies, and may go to great lengths to acquire kittens larger than their own. But do not cage the queens. It may seem convenient to box up the mothers with their litters, but the lack of exercise may lead to constipation and other troubles. A queen does not like using a tray close to her sleeping box and she likes to walk around at will. Her general health is the better for it and that means a good supply of milk and least work for the owner. When several litters are housed in

KITTENS AND BOTTLE FEEDING

Right: 'Our plates of food are coming'. Mingchiu kittens aged 9 weeks. *Below:* A 6-day-old taking his bottle. Note the way in which the kitten and the bottle are held; the level of the milk in the bottle is only just above the level of the mouth, no more.

29

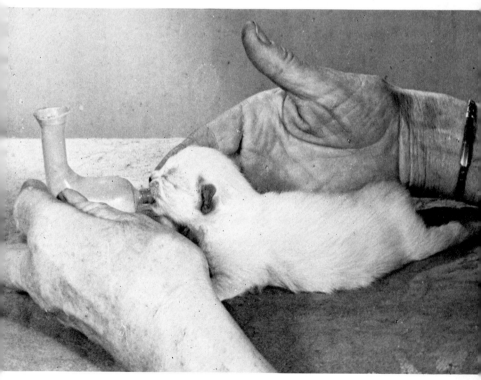

30

31

32

THE BACKGROUND

Above: Mingchiu Trivia, a Seal-pointed Shorthair carrying the genes for Long-hair, Blue, and Chocolate. She produced kittens with short, long and inter-mediate coat lengths, and the points were, Seal, Blue and Chocolate, but the type was poor for Longhairs, see p. 64. *Below:* An early Mingchiu Blue-pointed kitten lacking good demarcation between nose and forehead (cf. Colour Photo-graphs I-V, and Photograph 11).

33

34

Above: Mingchiu Mirabelle, a Chocolate-pointed prize-winning Siamese, with her litter of pure Siamese kittens. Contrast the type with that of Colourpoints and with the shorter face in Photograph 31. *Below:* A male Seal-pointed Colourpoint with fair coat, short, well-demarcated nose, but undesirable large upright ears set too close together (cf. Photograph 33 above and Colour photographs I-V, Photograph 2, etc.).

35

36

PROGRESS IN TYPE OF LITTERS

Above: Litter aged 9 weeks from Briarry Roxana, 1960, one Blue-point, five Seal-points, they were best Longhaired litter at Exeter, 1960, but the type is not good; contrast the noses and top of head with those in the kitten below. *Below:* 1968 Mingchiu kittens at 9 weeks showing the great improvement in type upon those shown above.

one room it may be convenient to have barriers betweeen the litters which will keep the kittens separate when small and let the mums come and go as they please. If there is any chance of litters being mixed, mark the kittens with lipstick in the ear. Here the mark remains for a few days, but marking the tummy with lipstick needs daily renewal because the mothers lick it off.

At Snuff's next litter she had milk of her own, but would she feed her new-born kittens? No! They were not so large, nor so impressive as a short-haired blue in the kitchen! All her energies and ingenuity were expended towards getting to the kitchen to feed that which did not need feeding. She was adamant, so again a foster mother was required to rear her very nice Colourpoints. She never looked at them again and soon was calling for a mate. At her third kittening, it was a 4-month-old kitten in a garden pen that took her fancy, but this time she did not win. Her kittens were bottle fed and for 12 hours after their birth she was shut up with her heart's desire, the 4-month-old male. In the morning she was much chastened after his rough biting and sucking, and she was then shut up alone for a further 12 hours during which her milk piled up. Then, in the evening, she was permitted to go to her own kittens, and she meekly crept into her box and fed them, and after that reared them perfectly. A little psychological and not veterinary treatment was required. But there is a moral to all this : never let a queen play about with other cats' kittens before her own are born. It stimulates the bigger-better-kitten complex.

At birth Colourpoints are white or cream in colour with pink noses, foot pads and ears. In a few days pigment forms in these parts (Photograph 30), and gradually the new hairs growing, as size increases, demarcate the 'points', the nose, ears and the middle of the face, the feet, legs and the tail. The mask spreads gradually, and in males the dark colour of the ears almost joins with that of the face but it takes two years to spread (Photographs 1 and 21). In females the mask is always less extensive. If there are seal and blue-points in a litter, it may not be possible to distinguish them for certain under the age of three weeks. And the same is true of Lilac and Chocolate-points together in the same litter. But if there are Chocolate and Seal-points in one litter, the distinction is clear from birth, the Chocolates being much whiter and pinker than the

Seals. Lilac-points can similarly be distinguished from Blue-points at birth.

The apparent type of kittens changes with their age. At first all ears are small and usually set pleasingly on the head (Photograph 8), the face is round and the nose may or may not be as one would wish. But noses that seem fine to start with may elongate in late kittenhood, and noses that are too straight at 6 to 8 weeks may shape up later and become well-demarcated from the forehead and entirely 'good type' in the end. After the baby prettiness comes a lanky and unlovely stage with a gawky appearance, large ears (Photographs 4–6), upright and pricked (Photograph 4), and the breeder may despair of any of them being any good. But the body then grows to fit the ears, the face and body fill out, and the gawkiness may or may not pass. The kitten in Photograph 5 became the champion in Photographs 17 and 18.

At first all kittens of a litter may be much alike in appearance, and the potential winners of the show bench, in litters of well-bred kittens, can usually not be picked out until the age of at least $3\frac{1}{2}$–4 months, possibly much older. Coat length may come early or late, it depends upon the inheritance and the weather and time of year. Good type in kittens depends very much on their parentage, and the chances of breeding a top flyer from parents both of which are champions is much greater than from parents which are less good in type. But in any case the finest typed kittens are very few and far between, and consequently are very much prized for future breeding (Photographs 2, 3, 6, 8, 9, 23). There is considerable variation in type among kittens from the same parents. One litter may contain one or even two outstanding kittens and the next two or three litters may contain none (Photographs 35, 36).

Some practical matters may be noted for the assistance of inexperienced breeders. First, how do you know when your queen is calling? This may be very obvious, but it may not be so. The voice is not so penetrating or loud as that of a Siamese, but usually the sounds are unmistakable. The cat wants to go out, to wander, and goes off her food, sometimes having eaten much more than usual just before the obvious signs of calling set in. The period may last a week or more, and the most propitious time for mating is about the third day when the call is at its height. But so often things are not like this. Some Colourpoints call only for one or two days, and the signs are best read by a male cat and may pass unnoticed by a human. Such females may be mated regularly by males who live with them, but they are obviously very difficult to get mated by a male living at a distance. Sometimes a female knows when she is about to call before her owner does, and she may see to it that she gives everyone the slip, later returning home mated and before her noisy period begins. A journey, a strange male and strange surroundings may put a queen off call entirely, or she may be just unco-operative. Or with a keen and understanding stud cat success may be achieved at the first attempt.

If a queen has not been successfully mated, she may start calling again in a fortnight, particularly in the spring, and go on like that repeatedly, to the detriment of her health. Or she may not call again for some months. When there is difficulty in getting a queen into kitten for the first time, it is as well to let her be mated by any cat, an alley cat of her own choice if need be, and for the next litter she will probably be more amenable. Whether the mating has been successful or not, the queen may go on calling until the end of the period, the length of which is normal for her. Continued noise does not mean that the mating has been unsuccessful, but sometimes a noisy caller may quieten down at once after a successful mating.

Immediately after a successful mating the queen will scream, roll on the ground and lick herself, and may chase the male away. The owner of a stud Colourpoint should watch the pair, because unless the act is watched there is no knowledge as to whether it has been achieved. But if the queen is unco-operative, the best that can be done is to leave her for a few days with the male and hope for the best, because no one can watch the activities for 24 hours a day. If she hides by day she will usually come out at night.

During pregnancy the cat should receive just as much food as she will take, increasing the meals to three per day besides a milk mix (see above), but do not feed in between meals or indigestion may be caused. The duration of pregnancy is usually 63 to 65 days. About a fortnight before the kittens are due the queen should be introduced to her kittening box, and it is important that she should be satisfied with it. A useful size is 18" × 18" with a pop-hole a few inches above the floor level, and a lid that can be removed or opened. The box should be closed to start with, and it can, with advantage, have a small rod fixed along the walls some 2 inches off the floor so that the mother cannot accidentally squash a very young kitten by leaning on it against the sides. Mother cats have supreme faith in their young getting out of the way when they lie down, and this the little ones are adept at doing, but only after the age of a few days. Plenty of paper should be put in the box, and the queen will dig in it and tear it to bits about five days before the kittens are born. Do not let the queen wander the week before kittening, or she may find some inviting coal hole or garden shed, or set her heart on someone else's perambulator as a potential site for kittens. But do not cage her, she needs all the exercise and normal freedom she can have.

It is best to be with your cat at kittening, but do not interfere unless you are quite sure that you know what you are doing and that the cat trusts you. Do not be too impatient, and keep the lid of the box shut, except for inspection. She may produce the first drops of discharge the day before the kittens are born. The birth of the first kitten of a litter may take time, and if it is a first litter, the cat may or may not get momentarily worried. Two things should be watched for. When the kitten is free, the mother will lick it and break the transparent membrane which may cover the head, if it has not been broken during the birth. It is essential that this membrane be broken at once so that the kitten can breathe air. Next, do not let the mother wander about with a kitten dangling, before the placenta or afterbirth is produced. This may not become free from the womb for a little time after the baby is born, and no great tension should be exerted on the kitten by the cord, or fatal injuries may be caused. If the queen is very restless, and usually she is not, then an understanding owner can save the kitten by holding it until the placenta is free. The mother will then proceed to eat the placenta. Watch that she does this, and that she does not eat too much of the cord, and thereby injure the kitten. Watch too if a kitten should be produced and the placenta left behind inside. At the end of kittening you should know, for choice, whether all placentae have been produced. If one is known to be still within, the mother should be taken to the vet at once, where she can easily be treated, and she will return and settle down; but otherwise she may not lie down and may become very ill, her temperature will rise, she will produce no milk, and unless attended to she may die. A few cats take no interest in the placenta, and then it is necessary to sever the cord with scissors which have been dipped in boiling water. The cat's mouth is not sterile when she severs the cord, but all needless risks of infections spreading up the cord from the cut end, which may lead to death of a kitten in a few days, should be avoided.

The time interval between the birth of one kitten and the next varies considerably. A second may follow the birth of the first in a few or in some twenty minutes. The whole litter may be born within one or two hours, or it may take very much longer. If the births are slow, the queen may settle down and feed those that are born, but she may be restless until all are free. If she is restless, tossing herself about, it is sometimes desirable to park the babies on a blanket over a warm bottle, leaving her perhaps one to keep her interest centred on the box, and give her the lot when kittening is over. Be in no hurry to summon a vet because your queen is slow in kittening. To speed her up may spell disaster. And do not worry if kittens arrive tail first instead of head first, the usual way round. But prolonged labour with no results calls for expert assistance.

Some time after all kittens are born, not at once, remove the wet paper and settle the family down on clean paper, several layers so that it is soft to lie on, but do not put in a blanket, or make the bed too soft. Kittens can easily be squashed if they sink into a soft substratum, or if their claws, all long at birth, catch into woven material. Claws slip on paper. Later, when the kittens are a few weeks old, blankets can be used with safety. Do not disturb the queen. She may care for a good drink of milk, egg-white and glucose (see p. 94), but otherwise let her settle and sleep and feed the young. If she will not settle down, if she gets in and out of the box, and wanders about refusing to lie down, either something is amiss inside or she has no milk. Do not hesitate, give the kittens a warm bottle or an electric pad under a blanket and leave them arranged so that they can move away from too much heat if they wish, and take the queen to the veterinary surgeon. Some simple treatment will put her right.

Occasionally a queen with nothing organically wrong with her at all refuses to settle down and feed her kittens, and follows the owner about. In such a rare case I have put a small temporary cage round the cat and her kittening box and given her a sedative (pheno-barbitone), also reducing the light in the room. There being no-where else to sit the queen sits with her kittens, they suck her as she becomes drowsy, so establishing the milk flow. After each meal she was freed to walk about the house and soon the cage could be dispensed with.

Do not move the position of the box in which the queen has kittened. If you do, she may decide she does not like the untrust-worthy box, and start carrying her newborns about, dumping them in various places where they will get cold or die. If your cat does this sort of thing after kittening it is a sure sign that you have not been treating her properly. She must have access to her box before-hand and she must be satisfied with it. Often I give my queens a choice of boxes.

Sprinkle the kittens and the box with G-Hex at some convenient moment, even if you believe your queen to be flealess. If she has any they will move off on to the kittens, and the eating of an in-fected flea at an early age may result in fully-grown tape-worms a month later, perhaps dozens in one kitten. Cures are difficult in young kittens and persistent tape-worms may kill the kitten or ruin its digestive capacities (see p. 124).

When the mother has settled down after kittening, respect her privacy and do not let strong light fall on the pop-hole. A watch must be kept to ascertain that she is feeding the kittens properly. If all is quiet the little ones are probably all right. If they cry repeatedly something is amiss; but have patience for a few hours, although see to it that none are being sat on. If the babies at first do not seem able to find the nipples, and if you cannot squeeze out any fluid from them, do not at once assume that she will have no milk. The supply may not become established for some hours after kittening, and if you leave the family alone the babies will suck and the milk will probably come. The kittens will be quite all right without food for some hours, and it is important that they have the colostrum secreted before the milk. Do not start hasty supplementary feeding that may not be required at all. But if the babies are noisy and there is no milk 8 or 12 hours after birth, it is as well to give them a bottle feed (see below p. 120), but do not repeat the feeding for another 5 hours at least. If you feed the babies too much they will be satisfied and not suck the mother, and she will not be stimulated to produce the wanted milk. But kittens must not be allowed to get weak from starvation. Some queens, as noted above, are habitually slow in coming into milk. Others can be brought into milk with a suitable injection, but in most cases Colourpoints make the most excellent mothers alone and unaided. If no sounds come from the litter except when the mother gets up, or when she comes back to settle down again, all is going well. But if the kittens are continually crying, then something is wrong, and if the temperature of the box is satisfactory, it is likely that there are feeding difficulties (see further below). Kitten boxes within earshot of the owner at night are a great convenience, because one knows with no trouble at all, whether the kittens are quiet or not.

Colourpoints can bring up their kittens in an unheated house in winter in England, the mother curling round them and keeping them warm. But this is not the best arrangement. The kittens are warm until they want to walk about, and then it is too cold for them, although they may survive. It is much better to have a kittening box in a reasonably warm room, 60 degrees F, but not too hot. Whether extra heat is suitable inside the box depends on the cat. Some Colourpoints can only be described as fussy, and hardly leave their kittens for a moment. No box heating is then needed. But Briarry Roxana, for example, a most efficient queen, does not believe in spending one more moment inside her box than is absolutely necessary. She always has a good 'head' of milk on her, she feeds her brood rapidly, as from a bottle, she licks them, 'puts them to bed', and walks away. They can bawl if they like, she is unmoved—knowing that they are quite all right and will very soon be asleep. She goes for a long walk or sits in the garden watching birds, all more interesting than sitting in a dark box while babies sleep. She stays away for several hours and then returns to her job. But she trusts me to keep the box warm, and this is done by tying an electric pad to one side of the box so that the kittens can cuddle up to it if they like, and the mother can keep away from it. She has no need of extra heat herself with her long coat. If the

111

box is too hot the queen will not sit in it. Other females feed their young at very frequent intervals, and never seem to have much obvious milk because it is taken off by the kittens as soon as it is formed. It is such feeding that has given rise to the idea that kittens must be fed frequently.

Well-fed young kittens are asleep almost all the time. They are quiet unless disturbed, and the middle of the body is nicely rounded and turgid. An inadequately fed kitten is awake and wailing and its little sides do not bulge. Increase in weight normally is rapid. At birth the kittens may weigh $2\frac{1}{2}$–4 oz and the larger ones may put on 4 oz in weight in a week. If in doubt as to how kittens are doing, weigh them daily, either singly or all together. If they are not putting on weight as they should, something is wrong. If one kitten is smaller than the others, it may have difficulty in competing for a place at the milk bar with its stronger siblings. If this is so, then supplementary feed the little one (see p. 120) who may then catch up with the others. If you suspect that all is not well with the mother take her temperature with a thermometer inserted at least half an inch into the rectum and left there for $\frac{3}{4}$ minute. Her temperature should be 102 degrees instead of the normal 101·5 degrees for a non-nursing cat, and if you find it is more, then consult your veterinary surgeon at once. Great care should be taken over her food, which is best more finely divided than usual. The increase in quantity which she needs should be given as more cooked rather than raw meat. And do not give more milk per day even if she has a passion for it, but with other foods respect her choice. Indigestion must be avoided if a good supply of milk is to be maintained. Egg white, either alone or mixed with a little glucose, may be a help if a queen is inclined to eat more than she can manage.

A watch must be kept on the state of the nipples. Only some may be in use, depending on the size of the litter, but if one becomes blocked and a gland inflamed trouble will start. A bite from a kitten with teeth may initiate an abscess. At all times be on the look out for abnormal occurrences. If the queen cries out when the babies suck, or stands up to feed them instead of lying down, there is probably something wrong with the mammary glands or nipples or an abscess is forming in or near those parts.

37

38

SPRING IN AN ENGLISH GARDEN
Ch. Mingchiu Monique aged 6 years and Briarry Roxana aged 10 years pottering about free and enjoying the smells of plants and soil.

39

40

PARTS OF THE MINGCHIU CATTERY

Above: A bird's-eye view by a wide-angle lens gives extreme foreshortening of a house for one male and two females. Ch. Mingchiu Shan sits on an outside shelf, one female sunbathes upon the roof and the other on an outside bench. The door of the house is open

41

and the run is more extensive than can be seen. *Left:* The left-hand side of the house, showing windows and access to the roof by tree trunks. *Right:* The door is shut and the pop-hole open.

Inspection will show the cause of the trouble; a blocked nipple will cause swelling and a redness of the skin over the gland, or an abscess can be present, as a hard painful lump either in the mammary glands or outside them. Hot fomentations, using a pad of cotton wool and warm water and a heavy dose of antibiotic, such as Terramycin, may very soon relieve the condition. It is of course better to notice what is going wrong and put it right before the cat's temperature rapidly rises to something of the order of 106 degrees and her life becomes endangered. If your first aid is not quickly successful, consult your veterinary surgeon.

When the kittens are about three weeks old the lid of the box should be removed, or the mother will decide on a housemove for the whole family, and put them somewhere where there is more light. Kittens' eyes open any time between the fifth and the tenth day, and they suffer greatly if exposed to bright light too soon. Eye troubles are easily acquired, and young kittens should be kept in low light intensities until they can stand more. Any sticky or discharging eyes should be treated with one of the many antibiotics prepared for this purpose.

At $3\frac{1}{2}$ to 4 weeks the kittens will usually come out of their box to run about, tail upright behind, returning to it to sleep and feed. Do not be alarmed if their weight drops instead of gaining, although the feeding is adequate. For three or four weeks the kittens are becoming more and more active and are learning to eat and digest food from plates, their increase in weight per week is slowed down, or it may actually fall. From 9 to 10 weeks onwards the rate of increase is re-established. A 3-month-old may weigh 3 lb and a 4-month-old 4 lb, but there is much individual variation, and kittens weighing little do not necessarily make smaller adults. An adult female weighs between $6\frac{1}{2}$ and 8 lb and an adult male usually between 8 and 10 lb, but 15 lb is not rare. A start on feeding from plates or spoons can be made at the age of 4 to 5 weeks; but as soon as food is taken in that way, a litter tray must be provided close at hand, and the kittens will straight away learn to use it. The mothers do not care for cleaning up behinds after solid food is taken.

Sexing young kittens may be quite easy, especially if both sexes are represented in one litter, but this is not invariably so. Some

H   113 males can appear very like females to start with, and a mistake may easily be made. In the male the two openings beneath the tail are further apart than in the female, and for a few weeks there may be no more difference than this. Later the incipient scrotal sacs in the male make their appearance.

Male kittens usually grow faster than females, but it is not always so. The adult male is a larger heavier animal than the female. But at birth the sexes may be the same size and not infrequently one of the larger kittens in a litter is a female and not a male. A really large kitten of 5 oz birth weight is a calamity, because the mechanical trouble attending its birth is seldom survived.

It is not intended to give an account here of abnormal conditions in breeding which lie in a veterinary province, but it may be useful to note a few abnormal, though not infrequent, occurrences which can be looked out for by the breeder. Really healthy, happy and well-fed animals make the best breeders, but sometimes difficulties cannot be avoided, although mismanagement may make them worse. Termination of pregnancies can occur at any stage; and pseudopregnancies in which there are no embryos, and resorption of embryos are well-known phenomena. In the early weeks, a rolling and perhaps a howl for a moment, with or without a vaginal discharge, is a warning that something is not right. The chances of observing the moment when this occurs are small, and all that is known is that there is no pregnancy some weeks after mating. If this behaviour is observed veterinary advice should be sought. A red discharge from a queen believed to be in kitten calls for expert advice. Kittens born prematurely are frequently eaten, unless they are within a week of full term, and the eating may pass unobserved. Many of these troubles are due to infections in the genital tract which are not apparent in the cat who seems perfectly healthy, and expert advice should be obtained. Pregnancies may terminate with a discharge of white matter from the vagina, and unless this is completely put right, no further breeding may be possible; the sign is an evil one. The birth of kittens a week or a fortnight too soon may result from genital infections, or nervousness, and treatment is probably indicated before, and perhaps after, the next mating.

Sometimes kittens are born a few days early and are success-fully reared by the mother, with or without help. But if one or two kittens are born early, followed in a few days by the rest of the litter, the mother usually will not come into milk for the firstborn. They can be bottle fed until the mother can take over. The cause is probably some genital infection, and the queen should receive treatment or she will do it again. There is also such a thing as dual conception, resulting from eggs being fertilized on different days, maybe by different sires. Ovulation occurs in the cat at the act of mating. In such cases the kittens will be born on different dates, and mechanical and physiological difficulties ensue. For this reason queens should not be mated on many successive days, or at least 2 days should pass in between matings, even if she is very willing. When there are a few drops of red vaginal discharge or some fluid from a queen a few days before kittens are due, one fears the worst and hopes for the best. Nothing much can be done about it but wait and see. Normal kittens may or may not be born. Kittens born dead, either whole litters or individuals, may not be accounted for by mechanical trouble, and advice should be sought. Abnor-malities such as cleft palates, lensless eyes, kinked tails, etc., may result from too little vitamins A and D in the mother's diet. Single kittens which do not suck properly may have cleft palates and are doomed; or sometimes they are suffering from an infection which has spread up the cord from the cut end and that also means they cannot be saved.

Kittens which seem normal at birth and peter out in 1–4 days, in spite of plenty of available milk, indicate maternal infections which need treatment. The queen may appear to be perfectly healthy with nothing wrong with the genital tract that can be felt by a veterinary surgeon. Such an occurrence should be treated most seriously, and it may be best to give every queen in the cattery, and perhaps the males as well, an injection of streptomycin if such occurrences are not to be repeated by the same and other queens. Unnecessary losses of kittens may thereby be avoided and the expense of treatment is well worthwhile. All divergencies from the expected must be dealt with effectively if further breeding is to be successful.

The birth of abnormally large kittens, 5 oz or more, usually leads to difficulties. If the kitten becomes arrested when half way out, the mother can be helped by gentle manipulation when she exerts pressure to expel the kitten, but it must not be pulled by hand from without, because irreparable damage to the kitten will result. If a birth is very slow, or if the kitten arrives tail first and the head end is in difficulties, there is always a danger of death by suffocation as there is no access of air to the mouth by the time the placenta is detached from the mother.

When a litter is apparently thriving it sometimes happens that suddenly the kittens refuse to suck, although the mother has plenty of milk; or if they suck they tend to vomit, or their tongues may become ulcerated. This does not usually occur before the age of 4 weeks, but is not infrequent between 5 and 8 weeks. The queen should be given half a tablet of milk of magnesia at bedtime for several days, and perhaps a purge (teaspoonful of castor oil). Testing the milk with litmus paper may reveal acidity; milk of magnesia is appropriate treatment, or a daily tablet of sodium citrate may neutralize the milk acidity. Alternatively the queen may be taken off the kittens entirely, and they can be reliably fed from a bottle or from individual plates five times a day. A young queen who is exerting herself too much in feeding her first litter, becoming thin in the body, often produces milk of unsuitable composition towards the end of lactation, and the kittens do better without it. Ulcerations in the mouth start with local swelling, the skin becomes white and peels off leaving red, raw areas. These should be painted with T.C.P. several times a day using a soft brush, and small knobs of butter that have been mashed up with T.C.P. can be put in the mouth.

Sometimes a whole litter or single kittens show signs of indigestion at 5–8 weeks of age (vomiting, loose motions, etc.). If you know that your plate feeding is blameless it is better to take the mother away and plate feed entirely (see next chapter) when the kittens should at once return to normal. If they do not, even when soothed by raw egg white given several times a day, it may be best to give Nuvamide, or other prescription from your veterinary surgeon (see next chapter).

Cats used for breeding often acquire scratches at the time of mating. Sometimes the male will bite the neck of a difficult female so hard that he breaks the skin. Such lesions are easily treated by pouring a few drops of hydrogen peroxide on to the raw place, and repeating the application until the skin is dry and healing.

14. Feeding kittens and bottle rearing

Kittens that are very well fed by the mother are not easy to feed from plates until 5 weeks or so in age, but if the mother is not doing very well, a start with a milk mix can be made at three weeks and the kittens can be independent by five weeks. Normally it is better to leave them with the mother until the age of eight weeks. The feeding of kittens needs endless care because indigestion is easily acquired and it not always easy to cure. But by taking trouble there never need be any kitten indigestion.

A beginning can be made usually between 4 and 5 weeks of age. A teaspoonful once a day of the kitten egg-white mix (see p. 94) makes a good start, and can be given from a spoon or from a small individual pot or plate. Something of the right size and heavy is the best, otherwise the kittens upset everything before they have learned the art of tidy lapping (Photograph 16). By 5 to 6 weeks they should be taking the milk mix twice a day, but more often if the mother gives up feeding them, as rarely occurs. The kittens at 5 weeks should be taking a very small amount of scraped meat (see p. 93), only about as much as will lie on a sixpence to begin with, and fine cut rabbit (or chicken) for the second meal. Four small meals a day, two of the milk mix and two of meat, are enough while the mother is still feeding the kittens. It is essential to keep the meals small.

If a mother stops feeding the kittens at 7 weeks they should have five meals per day, two of meat, cooked and raw, and three of the milk mix, the first meal being as early in the morning as convenient and the last just before going to bed. At eight weeks of age the most enthusiastic mum should be removed, leaving her with the kittens at night, but not in the daytime, for a few days before this. Kittens eat and lap at very different rates, and it is useful not only to give individual plates (Photograph 16) but to see that each kitten gets what is prepared for it. Or, if several feed off

118

one plate, the amount put out should be minimal, and when the plate is empty the kittens that feel not full enough can be given more in private, away from the gluttons. From 7 to 9 weeks of age the kittens thrive on 4–5 meals a day, the quantities of food being kept well in check because some will probably overeat if they get the chance. At 9 to 10 weeks a sudden inability to digest as much milk as before sets in, and the milk mix must be given only twice and then once a day. This is a very critical age for feeding and one in which trouble starts for the unwary.

Indigestion or diarrhoea may stem from simple overfeeding, or from feeding 'match stick' (p. 93) meat too soon instead of scraped meat, or from giving too much milk mix, or from catching cold by running about in floor draughts, or from internal infections. Great cleanliness of surroundings and litter trays is essential and do not let young kittens help themselves from plates of food prepared for adults. If in trouble, do not treat with antibiotics for supposed internal infections until you are quite sure that your feeding is not at fault. If you give antibiotics and there is no improvement, then your feeding is probably not right. Mingchiu kittens are weaned on to scraped horsemeat, beef or whalemeat and cooked rabbit, using the egg-white milk mix to start with and the M.O.F. mix (see p. 94) from about 9 weeks onwards. Complan can be used; kittens like it at first, though they soon tire of it but will then take half Complan and half egg-white mix. Complan is very useful because of its digestibility, but it must be given only with plenty of other foods or a condition of rickets rapidly develops. Any sign of impaired ability to run and jump is a warning that the food is unbalanced, and prompt appropriate action reverses the disorder very quickly.

Never feed kittens in between meals at any age. When there is slight trouble with digestion in kittens, caused by overeating, etc., it is useful to cut down the quantity of food given; to give a pipetteful of liquid paraffin at night and so hasten the removal of the offending matter; and to soothe the interior by giving teaspoonfuls or half teaspoonfuls of egg-white several times a day, or put some lightly whipped egg white on top of the meat at meal times. If a kitten has been vomiting, leave it unfed, quiet and warm for some hours, or for the rest of the day if its temperature is normal (101·5

119

degrees F), and give a little raw, slightly whipped egg-white next morning. The appetite may return rapidly, but be sure that the raw and cooked meat offered is finely divided, that too much milk is not being taken, etc. or the undesirable condition will return. If you cannot cure your kitten's indigestion within a very few days go to your veterinary surgeon for treatment, because the kitten will otherwise become emaciated and cease to grow. Remember that feeding 6–10 week olds is very critical and great attention must be paid to it if troubles are to be avoided. But if your kitten vomits and shows a sudden rise in temperature (103–106 degrees F) go to your veterinary surgeon with the least possible delay, and isolate all associated kittens.

If bottle feeding is necessary a suitable small feeding bottle must be used which is made for the purpose. It is curved, open at one end for cleaning and filling, and carries a teat at the other end, the teat in fact being usually the rubber valve made for cycle tubes. The teats can easily be renewed by replacing on the glass nozzle. The teat should have a hole in it of just the size to allow drops of milk to escape when the level of the milk in the bottle is a little above that of the teat. If the hole is too large a jet of milk will flow from the bottle, as from a tap, and if it is too small the milk cannot be sucked out by the force that a kitten can apply to the teat. The size of the hole should be carefully adjusted by experiments with water. The milk mix should be prepared as noted on p. 94 and the bottle sterilized before each feed. The mix should be warm, but not hot, much cooler than a 'hot drink'. Holding the bottle of milk against the skin of one's face below the nose is a good way of testing the heat, which needs to be just right or the feed will be refused by the kittens. An easy way to warm a kitten's bottle of milk, which has been filled by a sterilized spoon from the prepared mix in the fridge, is to have a piece of wire netting in a saucepan of hot water and stand the bottle on this momentarily, with the teat above water level. If everything is arranged just so, bottle feeding is no trouble.

To feed a kitten, place him on a warm cloth on a table in front of you. Raise the head and when he cries insert the teat into the mouth and against the upper jaw, gently steadying his head (Photograph 30). Keep the level of the milk in the bottle not too

120

XII THE NEWER COLOURS
Above: A Lilac-pointed Colourpoint, Mingchiu Sulafour, whose good type has resulted from 11 years of planned breeding.
XIII *Below*: Mingchiu Lilak, the first Self-lilac Longhair, a variety which is homozygous for Blue and Chocolate.

XIV THE NEWER COLOURS
Above: Lilac-pointed and Self-lilac Longhair kittens, Mingchiu Sulafour (left) and
Mingchiu Bini (right).
XV *Below*, left: Chocolate-pointed female, Mingchiu Vanessa at 8 months.
right: Self-chocolate Longhair female, Mingchiu Koca at 12 months with Mingchiu
Danladi, 8 months below the table, with intensely orange eyes.

high over the level in the teat, so that you do not cause too much fluid pressure. As the warm milk drips into the mouth the kitten will swallow, he will stop trying to move his head away, and will suddenly suck vigorously. When the kitten has taken all he wants he will let go of the teat, and it is most important not to overfill a kitten by force. Let him take what he wants and no more. Do not hold his head on to the teat. Replace the kitten with the mother, or keep him warm until you have fed the next, in order not to get muddled as to which kittens have been fed and which have not.

If need be, it is very easy to rear kittens entirely on a bottle from birth, and to do it without destroying the owner's sleep at night. Never give more than 5 feeds per 24 hours. It is quite needless to feed three-hourly, and such practice usually produces indigestion in normal healthy kittens which spells their end. For the first three days the kittens can do with a feed at 3–5 a.m., but after that age they will sleep soundless, from last thing at night, 10.30 to 11 p.m., until 7 a.m. or so, the remaining feeds being evenly distributed during the day. Let them sleep in the early morning and feed them when they cry. Motherless kittens can at first be kept in a small closed basket, on a pad of cellulose wadding which partly covers an electric pad running at its coolest. Right over the pad is too hot for the babies, and they will collect at the place where the temperature is most comfortable for them. Clasp the lid in order to avoid all interference by adult cats.

After each feed dab the behinds with cotton wool; the kittens will all perform to order, but do not hasten them, and usually they will not soil the box, at any rate to start with. Normally the first bright yellow faecal mass is produced 24 hours after feeding starts. This is repeated daily, but if the interval is two days and the product soft and normal, do not worry. Only if you are sure there is real constipation should you give one drop of liquid paraffin with a feed. I have bottle reared many kittens and have never had occasion to give any liquid paraffin. If kittens get themselves or each other in a mess, or if they get their fur wet on tummy and back legs, it is necessary to clean them carefully as for human babies, and dry off with talcum powder or skin troubles will ensue.

Kittens managed in this way will sleep without moving for 7 hours or so in the basket, but 5-hourly feeding is suitable timing.

121

When the mother has some milk, but not enough, it is useful to give one, two or three bottle feeds per day, and the mother will look after the nights and the washing of the kittens. (Photographs 25–28). Actually the washing of bottle-reared kittens when they reach the age of 4–9 weeks is much more trouble than the feeding. They get their faces in a mess at meal times and need careful cleaning after every meal in order to avoid spoiling the fur and getting eye infections. Sometimes a disappointed mum with no kittens can be left to do some washing at this age, but it is unsafe to leave her enjoying herself with tiny kittens because she may sit on them. From the age of 8–9 weeks the kittens learn to wash their own faces properly.

Never bottle-feed unless you are sure that it is necessary. Well fed kittens in charge of the mother are actually difficult to feed from a bottle. However, it must be remembered that hungry kittens need some initial persuasion to suck from the unnatural object, but as soon as they get the idea they are very pleased to see the bottle (Photographs 25–28), or to suck from it before the eyes are open.

15. Worms and inoculations

Two types of parasitic worms should be recognized and dealt with by cat breeders: roundworms and tapeworms. While much information of an imprecise nature has been known for a long time about these pests, it is only quite recently that a proper study has been made of the life cycle of the roundworms.[1] These worms, several inches in length when adult, may be infrequent in kittens, but if their presence is made known, the kittens should be wormed under veterinary supervision. The kittens will then remain immune from further infection for some months. The initial infection in kittens is intra-uterine in origin, and therefore it is essential that the breeding queens should be free from worms before pregnancy begins, or newborn kittens may be already infected. It is unwise to give worm treatment during pregnancy. The young worm may or may not make an excursion through the tissues of the kitten before establishing itself in the intestine. In puppies there is always this excursion. The eggs of the roundworm also pass out with the faeces of the adult cat or kitten. They are very small, and the egg shells are incredibly resistant to desiccation and even to strong chemicals and disinfectants, which do not penetrate the shell, even on total immersion for a long time. The eggs blow about in the air, or they can be licked up off the fur, and are easily swallowed. In the stomach the eggs hatch out into a minute larvae, which then makes an excursion through the bloodstream, liver and lungs and back to the intestine where the worms become mature. After the age of a few months a kitten previously cleared of round worms can become reinfected when a period of immunity is past.

Tapeworms are a much greater menace than roundworms in certain districts, where infected fleas abound, and are a real danger

[1]Warren, E. G., 1967, '*Toxocara* and *Neoascaris*, Studies on Morphology, Development and Migratory Behaviour'. Ph.D. Thesis of the University of Queensland, and shortly to be published.

to small kittens. Infections may be extremely heavy, the bulk of the growing worms filling much of the intestinal space. In time the mature segments of the worms will appear in the faeces, but long before that the kittens may become thin, show impaired appetites, loose motions, etc. If the apparent indigestion cannot be put right by attention to the diet, or treatment for indigestion as such, a tapeworm treatment is essential if the life of the kitten is to be saved. The younger the kitten the more difficult it is to give a safe treatment, and the attempt should be made under veterinary supervision. Great pains should be taken to avoid all tapeworm infection of kittens by absolute control of fleas.

The tapeworm utilizes two hosts for the completion of its life cycle. The adult tapes in the cat or kitten produce enormous numbers of minute eggs, again with resistant shells, which pass out with the faeces and can blow about and lie dormant for a long time. An intermediate stage of the worm lives in the flea. While the life cycle of the parasite has long been known, that of the flea in all its details, has only recently been worked out.[1] An adult female flea can live unfed for up to 17 months. She needs a blood meal before copulating and again before egg laying, thus no breeding is possible entirely away from the host, the cat or kitten. The female lays some 400–500 eggs which drop to the ground and hatch out in a slightly humid atmosphere. The larval stage of the flea, a minute maggot, lasts for from 1 to 24 weeks according to the temperature and humidity. The maggot feeds on dust particles containing organic material. Early naturalists fed them on the 'bran-like substance which sticks to the comb when puppies are combed' to which organic refuse was added. The latter is provided by the female flea 'which during her interminable meals, squirts out quantities of undigested blood through the anus.'[1] It is impossible to rear fleas if the iron content has been extracted from the blood fed to them. The larva spins a silk cocoon, pale brown in colour. Within it the pupal stage may last for 2 weeks or over a year, without feeding, waiting for the outside stimulus, a vibration caused by the footfall of a passing cat, and bursts out within a split second. The flea thus reaches the cat. If an accident happens to the flea of

[1]Rothschild, M. and Clay, T. 1952, *Fleas, Flukes and Cuckoos, a Study of Bird Parasites*, i–xiv, 1–304 pp., 99 photos, 4 maps, 22 drawings, Collins.

being eaten by the cat or kitten, then the resting stage of the tapeworm is freed in the stomach of the cat or kitten and passes down to the intestine to become the adult tapeworm. It is clear that the cycle can be broken not only by careful attention to coats (p. 98) but by general cleanliness that will break through the rest of the flea's life cycle. No dusty undisturbed crevices should be permitted anywhere in a cattery or premises frequented by cats, and dry undisturbed litter, dried up vegetation and dirt should be put out of bounds for cats.

The roundworms and tapeworms parasitizing cats are host specific and cannot live in man, although the same species of parasite can occur also in the dog. These general types of parasite are found rarely in man, but the species are different, as are the intermediate hosts, and none has anything to do with cats.

No Colourpoint is safely launched upon its way without being inoculated against feline enteritis. Usually it is recommended by the makers of the vaccines that a first inoculation should be given at $6\frac{1}{2}$ weeks of age followed by a second in over two weeks from the first, because the time taken for immunity to develop is about 10 to 14 days. Young kittens are immune because they are taking in antibodies against the virus from the mother's milk. The kittens must be treated at such a time as to induce them to make their own antibodies as a protection against the disease. The giving of the first injection at an earlier age has been frowned upon because it is said that it might have little effect, the kitten still having a sufficiency of maternal antibodies.

It is worth putting on record some serious troubles that have been experienced with more than one make of vaccine upon Colourpoints, and the manner in which the disasters have been overcome. It is generally agreed that after an inoculation a period of a few days follows in which the susceptibility of the kitten to feline enteritis (panleukopenia) is actually increased, and that care should be taken not to expose the animal to infection during that time. Actually very many kittens of various ages from $6\frac{1}{2}$ weeks and onwards have succumbed to the disease, becoming ill 6 or 7 days after inoculation with one make of vaccine; many died and some were saved by intensive treatments. It was noted that there was a greater chance of recovery in kittens affected by the vaccine

125

when inoculated at 6½ weeks of age than at 8½ weeks. This means that at 6½ weeks the kittens were benefiting by the presence of maternal antibodies to a greater extent than at 8½ weeks. It therefore seemed desirable to increase the antibodies in the young kittens to a level that would enable them to live through the critical days after inoculation by whatever means. First inoculations were given of a half or quarter dose and at the age of 4½ weeks, followed by a half or a full dose at 5½ weeks, a full dose at 7½ weeks and another full dose at 9½ weeks. Not a single kitten succumbed to the disease, although this treatment is against the current recommendations concerning early inoculations. At the present time all Mingchiu kittens receive a half dose at 4½ weeks and full doses at 6½ and 8½ weeks and no trouble of any kind has been experienced for a number of years.

All adult Colourpoints, whether they be kept for breeding or as pets, should be reinoculated once a year against feline enteritis, and preferably in the late winter or spring when the disease is not about.

16. Postscript

The names of the many champions mentioned in the preceding pages have been included so that the verity of the statements made can be checked by anyone wishing to do so. But the impression should not be given that champions in this country grow upon every bush. Each one has been the best kitten selected usually from a large number of litters. Moreover championships in England cannot be won in a day. On three separate occasions and under three different judges must the aspirant win the open class and in addition a Challenge Certificate. Even the finest Colourpoints have only a limited number of days per year when they are looking their best and their coats are full.

That most of the Colourpoint champions have been bred in the Mingchiu and Briarry catteries is no accident; and the Mingchui cattery, owning at the present day the greater number of British Colourpoint champions, did not have a flying start in the quality of its first Colourpoints, few in number, acquired from the Briarry cattery.

The Mingchui cattery is not large; there is place for but seven stud cats used for the breeding of six different varieties, the four colours in Colourpoints and the two new Self-coloured cats, besides of course Black and Blue Longhair. The quality of the Mingchiu cats stems from their manner of breeding along the scientific lines given above, using the two methods: the so-called quick and popular method of selecting from Colourpoint to Colourpoint matings, favoured here as in many other countries; and the much more profitable, but slower, method of the judicious use of self-coloured carriers of the Colourpoint pattern to bring in the genes wanted for all the finer details of the Longhair type.

The 1968-9 show season came just twenty-one years after the initiation of Colourpoint breeding in the Briarry cattery; and what a coming of age it has been! In Britain Ch. Mingchiu Mudoba

(Colour photographs I, V), as kitten and as adult, made nine consecutive wins of his open class and was nominated for best in show each time; he was best Longhair kitten in show once and later best Longhair cat, as well as champion of champions. He stands on an equal footing with the best of the old established varieties of Longhair cats. Abroad the Mingchiu cattery headed the list of top scoring catteries breeding any varieties in Canada and the U.S.A. with ten regional wins for the season. There are now a number of Mingchiu Grand Champions. How gratified Mr Stirling-Webb would have been had he lived to see these achievements, which vindicate the effectiveness of using Persian or Longhair cats of other colours for the advancement of Colourpoints, as described above.

The life-long affection for each other of two cousins, Brian and Harry, gave origin to the Briarry cattery and to its name. On their untimely deaths, almost within a year, four of Mr B. A. Stirling-Webb's cats made their home in the Mingchiu cattery. Two have been of assistance to, but have not played an integral or indispensable part in, the breeding in progress, and the other two have been spayed and kept for sentimental reasons. In the fullness of time the flower garden in which the Mingchiu cats live will be empty and the aviaries of foreign birds silent (the cats think they are put there for 'their amusement') but all over the world breeders with understanding can breed the 'cats with the delightful temperament', which is the heading of the Mingchiu cattery notepaper. Year after year letters come, which joyously confirm this caption.

The Mingchiu cattery owes its name to two much-loved cats long dead: Ming, a very ordinary Seal-point Siamese, but my first breeding queen, and Chu, a Chocolate-pointed Siamese and founder of three generations of top-ranking cats. Having achieved my then ambition in producing wonderful eye colour and fine type in the Chocolate-pointed Siamese, and having sent some of these kittens to foreign lands, I fell in love with Colourpoints, which meant abandoning all I had built up. The descendants of Chu were spayed and space was found and acquired for the breeding of Colourpoints. But a fitting memorial will be left to my two Shorthair cats and to my first stud cat, a Seal-point Siamese of character by the name of Wong.

128

42

43

Above: A corner of a run showing wooden shelves and boundary walls of concrete (right) and wood (left) below the wire netting. Ch. Mingchiu Polo sits on the shelter for the trays, Ch. Mingchiu Mudoba sits on a stone table and a Self-brown kitten is on a shelf. These two males live amicably together although mature. *Below:* Another corner showing, in addition, the grass plot and wired in bed of *Nepeta* (Cat-mint) on the right.

Appendix:
Coat colour of cats and of other mammals

The colours, patterns and textures of the coats of Colourpoints and of other domestic cats are related in different degrees to those of the wild fur bearing animals. There are some which share the Longhair feature found in domestic cats. The Angora rabbits are a parallel, in which the coat can be three times the normal or wild type length. In both cats and rabbits this character is controlled by the recessive genes *ll* (see p. 34). Guinea pigs also can be long-haired. The Rex coat in rabbits is caused independently by one of three separate genes which are also recessive. Two different Rex (see p. 16) producing genes have turned up in recent years in domesticated cats in different parts of England and in Germany. Both are recessive, *rr*, and called gene 1 and gene 2. A Rex gene 1 cat mated to a Rex gene 2 cat produces only normal coated kittens carrying both Rex genes in the heterozygous state (see p. 22). The Rex genes can be associated with the characteristics of most, if not all, Shorthair varieties of cat.

The appearance of an animal is determined in part by its genetical make up and in part by the environment in which it lives, the typical structural features of each species being the result of a balance between these two attributes. If one or the other is drastically altered then the appearance of the animal, or of its progeny, is changed. The Red Deer of Scotland are a stable species in this locality with well-known features. But Red Deer removed from Scotland and transferred to New Zealand become appreciably unlike the parent stock in a few generations. They are larger with differently proportioned bodies. It is the selection pressure exerted by the environment in its entirety, that is by climate, food, other animals acting as predators or prey, augmentors or reducers of the food supply, parasites etc., which maintains the stability of the appearance of each wild species. Under domestication the selection exercised upon animals is, or may be, very different from that exerted by the normal environment; genetical changes may occur which are not eliminated by natural

I

selection. Protective coloration and camouflage are no longer of paramount importance, and colour varieties may turn up under domestication by a reshuffle of existing genes, and persist. The existing varieties of domestic cat have arisen in this manner. But many of these colours are repeated in parallel by many species or orders of mammals. The genesis of coat colour variations has been seen in the golden hamster during the last 30 years or so in which this animal has been domesticated. These colour varieties of hamsters are not known in the wild, and first turned up after a few generations of domestication. The coat patterns of domestic cats have turned up in a similar manner and have been developed by cat breeders. Only more recently have new varieties been created purposely on a genetical basis, as described on previous pages.

Coat colours are repeated in a parallel manner by many different species of mammals, either the full range or only some of the patterns. A study of the genetics of mice, cats, rabbits, etc. demonstrates the existence of similar sets of genes controlling colours in these animals, and, moreover, these genes exhibit similar dominance relationships to each other. Thus it is probable that the loci of these genes on the chromosomes of these several mammalian species is also similar, and that these genes are homologous from species to species. But, since the number of chromosomes (see p. 19) in different mammals is not the same, exact correspondence between colour patterns of one species and another is not to be expected.

Fullest information concerns the inheritance of coat pattern in mice. Here over 40 *loci* have been recognized on the chromosomes (see p. 19), each being associated with a related series of genes, known as allelomorphs, which are alternative to one another, such as c^s and c^b, the genes in cats determining the Siamese and the Burmese colouring respectively. And as well there are many modifiers which result in a continuous series of colour gradation in domesticated mice. In cats, as yet, the series of colour varieties is largely discontinuous. Modifying genes are present but have not been referred to as such in previous chapters; their effects have been noted, mainly in association with the features of shape collectively known as type. It is to be hoped that breeders will be discriminating enough not to produce a continuous series of colours and patterns and shape in cats as has been produced in mice.

There are four related series, or groups, of colour patterns in cats which are repeated in many other species of mammals. The usage of the higher and lower-case letters and hyphens below and in the table on pp. 134–5 is explained on page 134.

1. *The Agouti series AA* or *Aa*, dominant Agouti, *aa* Non-agouti. Agouti is the wild type coat, found typically in mouse, rat, vole, guinea pig, cat, dog, fox, badger, pig, etc. Each hair possesses a terminal or subterminal band of yellow, due to phaeomelanin pigment granules, the rest of the hair showing black or brown eumelanin pigment. Mutant genes determine whether the phaeomelanin band is lost, as in non-agouti coats, or extended on the individual hairs as in yellow coats. The Agouti character of hair is distributed among cats as noted on p. 16, see also pp. 134–5 below.

2. *The Brown series BB* or *Bb* dominant Black, *bb* Brown. The gene for black pigmentation *B* is always dominant over that for brown *b*, and only a *bb* animal is brown in appearance. This series occurs in many mammals, such as mouse, rat, deer mouse, hamster, vole, rat, pig, mink, cattle, sheep, horse, man. Both colour and shape of the pigment granules are affected by these genes, and the *b* gene affects eye colour also in some mammals. The recessive *b* seems to be the wild type in some mammals. In cats the Shorthair Chestnut, or Chocolate Brown, is homozygous for non-Agouti and Brown with the symbols, *aabb* (see p. 134), and the Longhair Self-chocolate carries the *ll* recessive genes for Longhair in addition, *aa bb ll*.

3. *The Albino series C.* This series controls the intensity of hair, eye and skin pigmentation. It occurs in cats, rabbits, mice, chinchilla, coypu, dogs, mink, fox, etc. At one end of the series is the *C*, or full colour, dominant and, usually, the wild type, and at the other end is the albino *c* lacking pigment in coat and eyes. The amount of pigmentation is reduced step by step, the yellow phaeomelanin being first affected and then the black eumelanin.

C full colour
c^{ch} Chinchilla (Silver)
c^{b} Burmese
c^{s} Siamese
c Albino

The Chinchilla gene removes the phaeomelanin from the agouti band, producing Silver Tabby in agouti cats ($t^b t^b c^{ch} c^{ch}$). It also slightly reduces the intensity of black, as in the Smoke cats with dark tipped hair over a lighter base. Further reduction of black in Burmese cats $aa c^b c^b$ gives a brown coat. Chinchilla is dominant over Burmese, but Burmese is only incompletely dominant over Siamese, $aa c^s c^s$, the $aa c^s c^b$ cats being lighter than $aa c^b c^b$ cats.

The genes producing the Siamese pattern in cats are similar to those in the rabbit, guinea-pig and mouse. Albino cats, if they really exist, are very rare. White cats with orange or blue eyes are determined quite differently by a dominant gene W producing white.

4. *The Dilute series D*. The intense colour D is always dominant over the dilute colour d. These genes, as in the C series, affect the intensity of coat and eye colour, but by a different mechanism, that of clumping together of the pigment granules rather than by a decrease in their number, as occurs in the C series. In cats the series so far recognized consist of intense colour D and the 'Maltese dilution' d, which causes so called Blue varieties of cat, rabbit, etc. In mice there are intermediate members of the series. A Blue Shorthair cat is thus $aa dd$ and a Blue Longhair $aa dd ll$. The D series occurs in mink, rat, mouse, cat, dog, fox, but not always the full series. Lilac is produced in both Shorthair and Longhair cats by the addition of Maltese dilution dd to a genotype containing homozygous brown bb. Thus Shorthair Lilac is $aa dd bb$ and Longhair Lilac is $aa dd bb ll$. Similarly Lilac-pointed Siamese and Colourpoint or Himalayan result from the addition of Maltese dilution to a Siamese or Colourpoint genotype, thus a Lilac-pointed Siamese is $aa c^s c^s bb dd$ and a Lilac-pointed Colourpoint is $aa c^s c^s bb dd ll$.

The Tabby series. The Tabby series found in cats is absent from most mammals, in contrast to the four series just considered. It consists of:

(i) The *Mackerel Striped Tabby* which is probably the wild type. It is dominant, TT or Tt, over the striped types of Tabby. A *Lined Tabby* is recognized by some as distinct from the Mackerel (see Robinson 1959, footnote p. 34).

(ii) The recessive *Brown Blotched Tabby* $t^b t^b$ probably originated in Europe from the striped cats and has spread from there.

(iii) The *Silver Tabby* is usually a chinchillated Blotched Tabby $t^b t^b c^{ch} c^{ch}$ giving the blotched areas a silver appearance.

(iv) The *Red Tabby* carries the sex-linked orange gene (see chapter 8), the colour made as rich red as possible by modifying genes. The Tabby allele is usually the blotched, so that the Red Tabby male is $t^b t^b O$ and the Red Tabby female $t^b t^b OO$.

(v) The *Abyssinian cat* is almost uniform agouti and appears to carry the wild type Tabby genes T^a and A, B and C.

There are some widely distributed series of colour determinants in mammals which are absent from cats or which are not certainly present. A *Pink-eyed series P*, different from the albino series, changes the coat colour as well as that of the eye and is uncertain in cats. An *Extension series E* either extends or diminishes the amount of eumelanin in the coat, with an opposite effect upon the amount of yellow pigment. Usually dominance and extension of dark pigment go together, causing coats to be uniformly dark, as in black rats and black rabbits, whatever the agouti genes present may be. There is ease of confusion between members of the A and E series. Dominant black in the E series occurs in mouse, rat, deer mouse, hamster, coypu, pig, dog, cattle, horse, sheep, etc. and has been claimed to be present in cats. In mice it has been shown that there are seven different genetical ways in which a black coat colour may be produced, thus great care must be exercised in interpreting insufficient data from breeding of cats and of other animals.

The *Orange (sex-linked) gene O*. This gene gives orange (red or yellow) coats in males O while in females it produces tortoiseshell when heterozygous $O-$ and yellow-red when homozygous OO (see Chapter 8). *Tortoiseshell* cats show a patchwork of orange, black and cream markings and are usually only female. *Tortoiseshell and White* cats carry the genes *ss* for white piebald spotting as well. These varieties occur in both Short and Longhair.

Some of the genetical distinctions between certain varieties of domestic cats have been noted on previous pages, but never the full genetical make up of these varieties, which indeed is unknown. The following list brings together the distinguishing genetical combinations possessed by varieties of domestic cats in so far as they have been elucidated.

The capital letters denote dominant genes, and their homo- or heterozygous (see p. 22) states are written as for White cats WW and $W-$, either of which gives the visible character. The lower case letters, such as aa Non-Agouti, ll Longhair, dd Dilute colour (Blue), bb Brown, $c^{ch}c^{ch}$ Chinchilla, c^sc^s Siamese colour pattern, c^bc^b Burmese, etc. denote recessive genes which only cause visible effects when homozygous, the heterozygous state being written as $l-$ etc. The dominant agouti genes AA or $A-$ are usually not written down in order to simplify the notation, but they are present unless the recessive aa is entered. Similarly the dominant Shorthair genes LL or $L-$ are not written down but are present in varieties not bearing the recessive ll. The hyphen indicates a heterozygous state, $W-$ or $c^{ch}-$, of either a dominant or of a recessive gene when one chromosome of a pair alone carries the gene. A cat invisibly carrying a heterozygous recessive gene is best described as a carrier. Only the gene causing orange (red-yellow or tortoiseshell) is sex-linked, and as explained in Chapter 8, the females are either OO or $O-$ when homo- and heterozygous respectively, but the male is always O because there is no fellow for the X chromosome in the XY pair of male sex chromosomes.

SHORTHAIR			LONGHAIR
aa	Black		$aa\,ll$
$aa\,dd$	Blue		$aa\,dd\,ll$
	Brown		
$aa\,bb$	Havana or	Self-Chocolate	$aa\,bb\,ll$
	Chestnut Brown	Longhair	
$aa\,bb\,dd$	Self-Lilac		$aa\,bb\,dd\,ll$
TT	Tabby Mackerel		$TT\,ll$
t^bt^b	Tabby Blotched		$t^bt^b\,ll$
$t^bt^b\,O$	Tabby Red male		$t^bt^b\,O\,ll$
$t^bt^b\,OO$	Tabby Red female		$t^bt^b\,OO\,ll$
$t^bt^b\,c^{ch}c^{ch}$	Tabby Silver		$t^bt^b\,c^{ch}c^{ch}\,ll$
T^aT^a	Abyssinian		
$T^aT^a\,O$	Red Abyssinian male		
$T^aT^a\,OO$	Red Abyssinian female		

$aaO-$	Tortoiseshell (females only)	$aaO-ll$
ddO	Cream male	$ddOll$
$ddOO$	Cream female	$ddOOll$
$aaddO-$	Blue Cream (females only)	$aaddO-ll$
	Red Self (similar to Red Tabby)	
	Chinchilla	$c^{ch}c^{ch}ll$
		$c^{ch}-ll$
	Blue Chinchilla	$c^{ch}c^{ch}ddll$
		$c^{ch}-ddll$
	Smoke	$aac^{ch}c^{ch}ll$
	Blue Smoke	$aac^{ch}c^{ch}ddll$
$W-$	White, blue or orange-eyed	$W-ll$
WW		$WWll$
$W-c^sc^s$	Foreign White	
WWc^sc^s		
SIAMESE		COLOURPOINT
aac^sc^s	Seal-point	aac^sc^sll
aac^sc^sdd	Blue-point	aac^sc^sddll
aac^sc^sbb	Chocolate-point	aac^sc^sbbll
aac^sc^sbbdd	Lilac-point	$aac^sc^sbbddll$
aac^sc^sO	Red-point male	aac^sc^sOll
aac^sc^sOO	Red-point female	aac^sc^sOOll
aac^sc^sO-	Tortie-point (females only)	aac^sc^sO-ll
aac^bc^b	Burmese	

Some of these colour varieties occur typically in both Long and Shorthair cats, such as the *Blacks*, *Blues*, *Tabbies*, *Blue-Creams*, *Creams*, *Tortoiseshells*, *Whites*, etc. But others are restricted to coat lengths. No Longhair *Abyssinian* or Shorthair *Chinchilla* or *Smoke* exist.

The *Dominant White* gene *W* gives the typical Longhair and Shorthair Whites with the type characteristics of these groups, see pp. 15, 16, 31. But this gene in combination with Siamese creates white cats with blue eyes and the type characteristics of this variety, in contrast to the typical Shorthairs and Longhairs. These cats in Britain are called '*Foreign Whites*' because the Siamese type is termed 'Foreign', see p. 16.

The *Colourpoints* or *Himalayans* are not simply a longhaired variety of Siamese as the genotype entered above suggests. Their Persian or Longhair type is controlled by most important modifying genes which determine the features of shape in which they resemble the typical Longhairs.

The American *Balinese* variety is a long haired cat with both colour pattern and shape of the Siamese but quite different in its modifying genes from the Colourpoint.

The *Birman* is another variety carrying the Siamese genes, and here the type structure is intermediate between those of Siamese and of Longhairs, and in addition the genes for white feet are present. White feet can be obtained in all domestic varieties, but selection has eliminated them from exhibition strains of domestic cats.

The difference between the Shorthair 'British Blue' with its round head and massive structure and the 'Russian Blue' (not geographically associated with Russia), with a differently shaped head and body and different coat texture, is again due to unanalyzed modifying genes. These varieties are quite distinct and are maintained so by selective breeding within each variety.

The *Tortoiseshell and White* varieties in both Long and Shorthair carry, in addition to the genes noted in the Table for Tortoiseshell, those for white spotting as well, *ss*.

The genetics of the *Manx*, *Bu-*, tail-less cats are not well apprehended. This structural feature occurs in many colour varieties of Shorthairs and sometimes in Longhairs. But the Manx features, in contrast to all those considered above, are not clear cut, and all grades from normal tails to tail-less kittens can be found in the same litter.

The *Red Tabby* and *Red Self* cats are similar in their major recognizable genes, and it is probable that the latter variety has arisen by selection from the former, many modifying genes being involved. The Red Self often lacks Agouti.

Among the Longhairs, the genes producing the Chinchilla hair characteristic are present in three varieties, the *Silver Tabby*, the *Chinchilla* and the *Smoke*. Much remains to be learned about the genetics of these and of other varieties of cats.

Although the several varieties of domestic cats listed above are probably characterized by the genes noted, it is clear that very many other genes referred to under the title of 'modifying genes' are at work in creating each variety in its entirety, that is conformation of body and texture and colour pattern of the coat. Fuller information will be found in Searle's *Comparative Genetics of Coat Colour in Mammals* (1968)[1] and in making the above summary this work has been freely used as being the most modern survey of the data. See also the earlier review by Robinson (footnote p. 34).

[1]Searle, A. G., 1968, *Comparative Genetics of Coat Colour in Mammals*, Logos Academic Press.

Index

Abyssinian, 16, 133
Adexolin, 95
adolescent, 43
agouti, 16, 131
albino, 131
Allbran, 95, 97
allelomorphic pair, 24, 130
Angora, 15, 129

Balinese, 15, 44, 136
behaviour, 75, 84
benzalkonium chloride, 101
Bicolour, 15, 16, 82
Birman, 15, 17, 44, 48, 68, 81, 136
birth, 108
Black, 15, 16, 52, 55, 131,
    Photographs, 15, 16, 20
Black and White, 67, 81
Blue, 14, 15, 16, 52, 55, 132, 135,
    Photograph, 14
Blue-Cream, 15, 16, 73, 135
Blue-point, 17, 55, 56, 135,
    Colour photographs III, VII,
        Photographs, 7, 8, 9, 11, 19, 22,
        23, 32, 37, 38
body, 31, 42, 46
body colour, 44, 45, 76
bottle feeding, 94, 104, 120,
    Photograph, 30
breeding, 20, 102
breeding difficulties, 114
brewer's yeast, 92
Briarry Bizbod, 43
Briarry Bruno, 65, 66
Briarry Candytuft (Ch.), 84,
    Photograph, 2
Briarry Cattery, 14, 43, 45, 53, 55, 62,
    67, 127

Briarry Euan (Ch.), 35
Briarry Far Neerah, 44
Briarry Jehane, 36, 43
Briarry Macsuch (Ch.), 65
Briarry Madre Decacaid, 66
Briarry Roxana, 56, 78, 111,
    Photograph, 38
Briarry Swashbuckler, 43, 65
Briarry Tromo, 41, 64
Briarry Uglia, 44
Briarry Ugly, 44
Briarry Zorab (Ch.), 79
"British" cats, 15, 16
Brown, see Self Chocolate Longhair
brown series, 131
Bubastis Georgina, 55
Burmese, 16, 131

cage, 77
calling, 106
Cats Magazine, 36, 51, 53
Cestarsol, 98
Chestnut brown, 16, 17, 131, 134
Chinchilla, 15, 55, 131
Chocolate, see Self Chocolate
    Longhair
Chocolate Point, 17, 42, 52, 57, **62**,
    135
Chocolate-point (pseudo), 61
chromosomes, 19, 44, 69
cleaning, 101
coat, 15, 31, 42, 45, 98, 129
coat colours, 129
Collins, Miss, 55
Colourpoint, 13, 15, 17, 56, 135
Complan, 94, 119
Cream, 15, 16, 73, 135
Cream-point, 73

6 1/2 ← 8 1/2